THIS IS
RE!

3

THE SCHOOL OF ST HELEN AND ST KATHARINE
FARINGDON ROAD
ABINGDON
OXFORDSHIRE OX14 1BE
TELEPHONE 01235 520173
FAX   01235 532934

Notes

The terms BCE (Before Common Era) and CE (Common Era) have been used throughout. Words printed in SMALL CAPITALS (first mention only) are defined in the Glossary on pages 132–134.

Although every effort was made to ensure that the website addresses were correct at the time of going to press, John Murray (Publishers) Ltd cannot be held responsible for the content of any website mentioned in this book.

The wording and sentence structure of some written sources have been adapted and simplified to make them accessible to all pupils, while faithfully preserving the sense of the original.

Orders: please contact Bookpoint Ltd, 130 Milton Park, Abingdon, Oxon OX14 4SB. Telephone: (44) 01235 827720. Fax: (44) 01235 400454. Lines are open from 9.00–6.00, Monday to Saturday, with a 24-hour message answering service. You can also visit our websites www.hodderheadline.co.uk and www.hoddersamplepages.co.uk

© Cath Large and Alan Brown 2004

First published 2004
by Hodder Murray, a member of the Hodder Headline Group
338 Euston Road
London NW1 3BH

Reprinted 2004 (twice), 2005, 2006

Artwork by Oxford Designers & Illustrators
Layouts by Fiona Webb
Cover design by John Townson/Creation
Typeset in 13/14 pt Goudy by Fakenham Photosetting Ltd, Fakenham, Norfolk
Printed and bound in Italy

A CIP catalogue record for this book is available from the British Library.

ISBN-10: 0 7195 7523 0
ISBN-13: 978 0 7195 7523 5

Teacher's Book ISBN 0 7195 7524 9

THIS IS
RE!

CATH LARGE

ALAN BROWN

General consultant Stephen Lavender
Adviser for Religious Education, Hertfordshire

3

Hodder Murray
A MEMBER OF THE HODDER HEADLINE GROUP

Contents

Final task	Key words	ICT opportunities	QCA links
• Express your identity as a concept map, a self-portrait, a maze, a poem or a wheel of life	• Identity • Orthodox • Ummah • Messiah • Bhavachakra	• Tape an interview • Word process and design graphics – as options for the final task	✓9A Where are we going?
• Write an essay comparing different religious beliefs about life after death	• Soul • Karma • Reincarnation • Shiva • Bet Chayim • Resurrection • Judgement • Akhirah • Barzakh	• Research websites and CD-ROMs • Edit and summarise key points using a word processing package	✓✓9A Where are we going? Sections on beliefs and practices about life after death
• Complete a pyramid summarising the main points in this unit, drawing together all your thoughts on the key question	• Agnostic • Atheist • Theist	• Set out, summarise and evaluate a survey on belief in God • Word process your own poem or song lyric with appropriate illustrations	✓7A Where do we look for God?
• Draw a concept map to show how science and religion agree and disagree and then analyse it	• Myth • Evolution • Creation • Theory	• Research websites on perspectives of creation – evaluate similarities and differences	✓✓9B Where did the universe come from?
• A card-sorting exercise to reflect on suffering and its effects on your own and others' belief in God • A personal response to the statement 'Suffering makes it too hard to believe in God'	• Natural disasters • Creation • Symbol • Justice	• Word process – could make a class display using images downloaded • E-mail support groups • Research other people who have overcome suffering • PowerPoint presentations • Research an organisation or an individual who works to relieve suffering • Word process a booklet	✓✓9C Why do we suffer? ✓✓7B What does justice mean to Christians in practice?

✓✓ close link
✓ part link

Contents

Final task	Key words	ICT opportunities	QCA links
• Express the conflict between good and evil in a PowerPoint presentation	• Satan • Karma • Moksha • Myth	• Search for newspaper headlines • PowerPoint – for the final task	A strong general unit underpinning many philosophically-based RE themes A good introduction to GCSE
• Summary task for Units 3–6: debate on reasons to believe or not to believe in God			
• Write a letter to a new teacher at a school in Jerusalem.	• Neve Shalom • Wahut al-Salam	• Research websites for information about Jerusalem – Jewish, Christian and Muslim • Virtual tour of Jerusalem	✓✓9D Why are some places special to religious believers?
• Compile two sets of commandments for people in their exercise of power over technology	• Gene technology • Embryo • Ethical	• Prepare and use a spreadsheet for 'Genes R Us' • Word process the final task on commandments	A strong general unit which raises ethical questions about religion in modern life
• Create a 3D image or computer graphic with commentary to represent the idea of a bridge overcoming a barrier	• Protestant • Catholic	• Record a commentary • Research websites on Mostar Bridge and Corrymeela community • Use computer graphics	A strong summary, using this theme to reflect on issues raised throughout the whole of this book

✓✓close link
✓part link

1 Who am I?

Your final question – for the big prize – 'Who **are** you?' Are you:

Who am I?

a) a member of a family brought up in the ROMAN CATHOLIC FAITH?

b) a set of unique DNA?

c) a Real Madrid supporter and keen footballer?

d) a prawn cocktail crisp fanatic?

YOU ARE WHAT YOU EAT

e) a softie who loves his pet rabbit?

f) someone who dreams of one day being prime minister or a successful businessman?

Outcomes   By the end of this unit you will:

- understand how and why IDENTITY is complicated
- evaluate ways in which you can make choices
- explain how religion gives some people identity and helps them make choices.

Literacy   Draw a concept map, write a self-portrait, design a maze for the journey of life, draw a wheel of life, write a poem.

Final task   This unit is about **you**, so you must decide. Each spread of the unit gets you thinking about one aspect of identity and gives you a different way of expressing your own: a concept map, a self-portrait, a maze, a poem or a wheel of life. How you sum it all up at the end is up to you.

Task 1A

1 Look up the word 'identity' in a dictionary and a thesaurus. Write down a definition to show that you really understand the meaning.
2 With a partner:
  a) discuss why the contestant is having such difficulty with this question about his identity. Is it because **all** of the answers are true?
  b) discuss which things he **can** change or control about his identity and which things he **can't**.

What about you?

- You are **unique**. There is no one else like you.
- You are also **complicated**. No one knows everything about you.
- You are also **changing** day to day, week to week, year to year.

But you are still you.

This unit is about you: who you are; who you'd like to be; and who you could be.

Task 1B

3 Draw a simple diagram of what contributes to **your** identity. Add more ideas if you can.

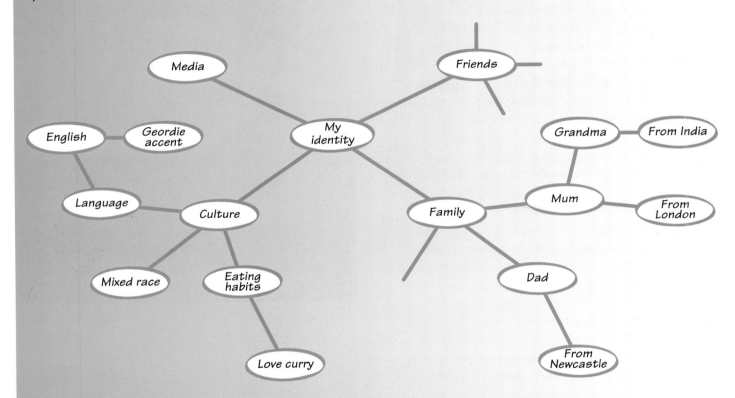

4 As with the contestant, there may be things about your identity that you think you can and cannot control (see Question 2). Write a description of yourself, highlighting:

- in red, the things you can control
- in green, the things you cannot control
- in yellow, the things you are not sure about.

Compare your answers with a partner.

● Am I...my looks?

When someone looks at you, what do they see? What do you want them to see?

Here are some self-portraits by famous artists. When an artist creates a self-portrait, they do not only try to show what they look like. They usually also try to tell you something more about themselves.

A

Frida Kahlo was in a tram accident that left her in a wheelchair for years.

B

Vincent van Gogh has his head bandaged because he had just cut his ear off in a fit of depression.

Task 2A

Choose the portrait you find most interesting.

1 Focus first on the physical appearance, what you can see. Describe the artist's external, physical features.
2 Now look deeper. Describe what else you can discover about the person from the portrait. For example, their feelings, character or experiences. Write down what aspects of the portrait give you these impressions.

C

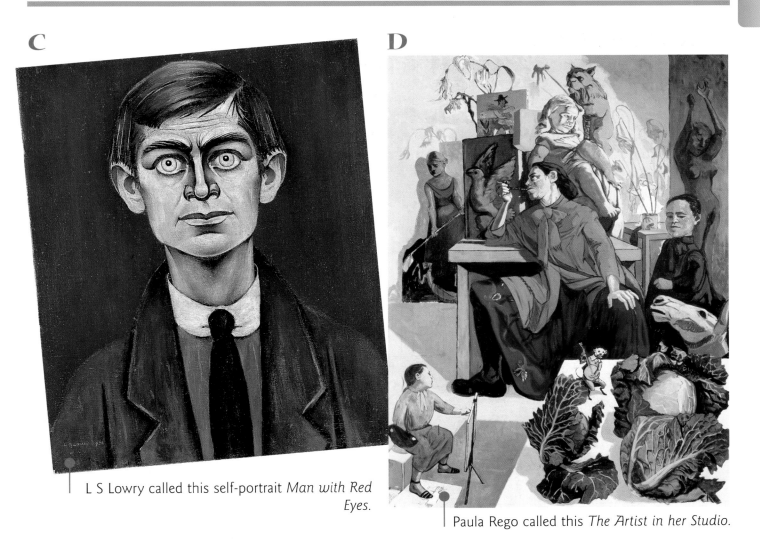

L S Lowry called this self-portrait *Man with Red Eyes.*

D

Paula Rego called this *The Artist in her Studio.*

Task 2B

3 Draw a simple outline of a body like this. On one side list words that describe the outer you (your physical appearance); on the other side list words that describe the inner you (your feelings, character and experiences). Number the words in each list in the order of their importance to you. Compare your answers with a partner.

Inner   *Outer*

4 Abraham Lincoln, a famous President of the USA, said that you can't help what you look like when you are born but 'every person can help what he or she looks like by the time they are 40'. What do you think he meant?

● **Am I...my relationships?**

Relationships and the groups you belong to are major influences that shape your identity – some in a good way, some possibly in a bad way. Some will be recent, some will have changed little since your childhood. Which relationships have the greatest influence on you? Which contribute to your identity the most?

The bewildered contestant on page 2 might have shown his relationships like this. Greater influences on his identity are closer to the centre.

Task 3

Do this exercise for yourself. Draw a circle with a dot representing you in the centre. You might find it helpful to draw several concentric circles in case some relationships have the same impact on your identity. Write the name (Mum, Dad) or role (teacher, neighbour) in the appropriate part of the circle to show the strength of the impact. Write a brief explanation of your diagram.

Am I...what I do?

Think of someone you knew very well but now no longer see. This could be someone of whom you were very fond. The person could have died or moved away. What is it you remember about that person?

Sometimes it is the things they did – their actions, their personal habits or routines – that people remember most clearly.

About my father

Alan Bennett is a modern author. He has written many plays for television, some of which have been about ordinary people – the things they said and did.

When his own father died, it was these things he remembered.

> *A few weeks after he dies, I go to Scotland to stay with friends by a remote loch in Morven. It is early evening when I arrive and they are out for the day so I sit outside the cottage in the last of the sunshine and make some notes about my father.*
>
> *He always washed up.*
>
> *He generally liked to be in bed before my mother and slept on the right side.*
>
> *He always wore black shoes.*
>
> *He often picked up stuff in the street – coins, naturally, but which pleased him out of all proportion to their value; nuts, screws, bits that had fallen off cars. Mum disapproved of this habit lest the things might be dirty.*
>
> *He had no smell at all, and when he died scarcely a grey hair; paleish blue eyes and a worn red face brimming over with kindness and pleasure.*
>
> *When he washed, he dried his face so vigorously that it squeaked.*
>
> Alan Bennett, *Telling Tales.*

Photo © Derry Moore.

Task 4

1 Discuss with a partner:
  How do you think Alan Bennett feels towards his father? Give reasons.
2 Make some notes in a similar way to the extract above about a person or a pet you love or remember.
3 Now make notes in the same way about yourself. What do you do – your habits and routines – that someone else would notice and remember? You might find it easier to write in the third person, as if you were writing about someone else: 'He/She does...'.

● Am I...my decisions?

Life is uncertain. We wonder what might happen tomorrow, next week or even in the rest of our life. Sometimes we lie awake and think. It can be exciting but it can be worrying too.

Mazes have been used for thousands of years to represent this uncertain life journey we are on. You can probably see why.

Mazes force you to make choices in direction. Some lead you to a dead end, some bring you to crossroads. Life choices are a bit like that.

Even everyday choices – what to wear when going out with friends, which team to support, whether to watch TV or do homework – can affect your identity. But there are some big decisions that can have a major impact on our lives. They shape the person we become. They determine our identity.

They can be choices about:

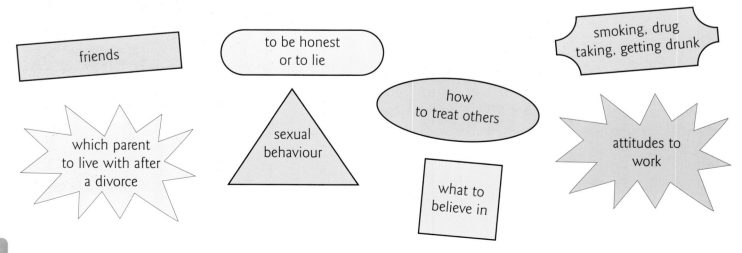

The maize maze at Sulleys Farm in England. It is made up of three kilometres of paths hedged by corn on the cob (the sort used for cattle feed).

friends

to be honest or to lie

smoking, drug taking, getting drunk

which parent to live with after a divorce

sexual behaviour

how to treat others

attitudes to work

what to believe in

Even wizards have identity problems!

At first, Harry Potter had no idea who he was. It was not until his encounter with Hagrid that he discovered the identity of his parents and the fact that he was a wizard. At the end of *Harry Potter and the Chamber of Secrets*, Harry has this conversation with Dumbledore:

'So I should be in Slytherin,' Harry said, looking desperately into Dumbledore's face. 'The Sorting Hat could see Slytherin's power in me, and it –'

'Put you in Gryffindor,' said Dumbledore calmly. 'Listen to me, Harry. You happen to have many qualities Salazar Slytherin prized in his hand-picked students . . . resourcefulness . . . determination . . . a certain disregard for rules,' he added, his moustache quivering again. 'Yet the Sorting Hat placed you in Gryffindor. You know why that was. Think.'

'It only put me in Gryffindor,' said Harry in a defeated voice, 'because I asked not to go in Slytherin . . .'

'Exactly,' said Dumbledore, beaming once more. 'Which makes you very different from Tom Riddle. **It is our choices, Harry, that show us what we truly are, far more than our abilities.***'*

Harry Potter and the Chamber of Secrets by J K Rowling.

Task 5

1 Either

a) In pairs, write down three big choices you might have to make in the future. You can get ideas from the opposite page. For each, describe two different outcomes that could be possible. Agree on which outcome would have the best effect on you as a person and contribute positively to your identity.

or

b) Design a simple maze to show the 'journey of life'. Here is an idea you could copy or develop. You could add signs to show crossroads (big decisions), dead ends (this will get you nowhere), road narrows (gets difficult), danger points (risky), one way (can't go back) and add an example of each from your own experience. You may need to write a commentary to go with your maze to explain how it relates to your life journey and the choices you have to make.

2 At the maze on page 8, guides stand on the bridges to help you if you get hopelessly confused or lost. And, of course, you can always change direction and learn from where you went wrong last time. Add to your list or maze ways in which you could get this sort of guidance and help in the real 'maze' of life's journey. For example, from older relatives or religious teaching.

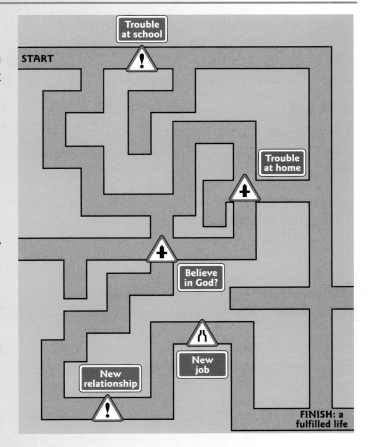

How does religion add to a Jew's identity?

This boy is becoming BAR MITZVAH. He is coming of age. Every Jewish boy goes through this ceremony age 13. There is an equivalent ceremony for girls called Bat Mitzvah.

He is carrying the scrolls of the Torah – the first five books of the Bible – which tell all the oldest Jewish stories and record the Jewish laws.

- To his head he has strapped the tefillin – a box that contains the words of the Shema: 'Hear, O Israel the Lord our God, the Lord is One.' The same words will also be placed in a box (a mezuzah) and fixed to the doorpost of his house.
- On his head and around his shoulders he wears the cap and the shawl (the tallit) worn by all Jewish men when they pray.

These external things help give identity to this boy. Doing the same things as others often helps our sense of identity. Can you think of examples in everyday life?

But there is much more to it than this. All these external features are reminders of past events, or important laws.

The Jewish traditions are full of ceremonies and symbols. They are part of the glue that holds Jews together. Here are a few more examples:

Shabbat

According to the Torah, when God finished creating the world, God rested. To remember this God commanded the Jewish people to observe Shabbat – a day of rest and worship every week. Shabbat begins each Friday evening at sunset. Every time Jews share in this ancient Shabbat tradition they are proclaiming their identity.

Circumcision

In the Torah, one of God's first commands was that Abraham and his family should be CIRCUMCISED. This would be a physical sign to mark out that they had a special relationship with God. To this very day almost all Jewish parents continue this tradition and take their male babies to be circumcised at eight days old.

The Passover (Pesach)

According to the Torah, Abraham's descendants became slaves in Egypt. Then God used Moses to lead them out of Egypt towards their new life in the 'promised land'. God commanded them to remember this event and relive it every year – eating the same food, and repeating the same rituals as they did on the night before their escape from Egypt. And they still do this.

These traditions have been very important to Jews because their history has been one of constant change and challenge. In 70 CE, their temple in Jerusalem was destroyed by the Romans and the people scattered all over the world. They lost their 'promised' land. In the Middle Ages, Jews suffered persecution by Christians who blamed them for the death of Jesus. In the 1930s, Hitler's fanatical hatred of the Jews resulted in the horrific persecution and cruel death of six million Jews – the Holocaust or Shoah.

But do these ceremonies and symbols still give identity to Jews today? Here is a family at their Passover meal (the Seder). What would they say?

Task 6

1 Imagine you are one of the characters and write a letter to Abby's unborn child. The subject should be the importance of ceremonies, symbols and actions in shaping identity.

2 Which family rituals and customs shape your identity? Special occasions? Places? People? Beliefs/rules?

Grandmother

When my husband was alive, we kept all of the traditions. We had both survived. In the camps, it was hard to keep believing in God. We said the PRAYERS we had been taught. We even made candlesticks out of bits of metal lying around the camp. Young Jonathan has not had his faith tested like me!

Father

I hated God for a while. I saw what had happened to my parents' generation. I even considered not having Jonathan circumcised. Then I went to Israel to work on a KIBBUTZ. It was just after the Six Day War and Israeli forces had recaptured the Western Wall – all that was left of the temple the Romans destroyed. The sight of men praying and weeping at that wall changed everything for me.

Jonathan

I am proud to be Jewish. There were times when I was younger that I kept a bit quiet about it! Now I'm in Year 12, my school friends respect my identity more and ask me questions like, 'Why is Shabbat special?', 'Why do you wear tallit in synagogue?'

Abby

To be a Jewish mother is so special. My husband and I do keep a Jewish home. I was given everything I needed for this when I got married – the Shabbat candles and the Seder dishes. My child will be born soon. If my child is a boy, I will have him circumcised – that is the tradition. We must do all we can to continue traditions in the future.

Mother

I have kept an Orthodox home all these years. The mezuzah on the door is a symbol that God is in our home so it really matters to me to bring up my family to keep the Jewish way of life. I was so proud to see Jonathan when he became Bar Mitzvah.

11

How does pilgrimage add to Muslim identity?

For Muslims, personal identity is part of a much bigger identity – the UMMAH, the worldwide community of Muslims, which knows no national boundaries.

The city of Makkah is a symbol of that unity. It is special for Muslims because it is the birthplace of their final prophet, Muhammad ☪. It is the site of the Ka'bah, believed by Muslims to be the first house of prayer on Earth. Once in their lifetime, every Muslim is supposed to go on hajj (pilgrimage) to Makkah, if health and finances allow.

A

Pilgrims throw stones at the pillar, which symbolises the devil.

B

A solitary pilgrim stops to pray on his way to Makkah.

C

All the pilgrims surround the Ka'bah to pray.

D

Malaysian pilgrims arrive at Makkah on hajj.

Going on hajj

Soofia and Karim are a young Muslim couple going on hajj. They have their special hajj visas (only Muslims are allowed to enter the holy city at this time).

There was just one more thing they had to do for themselves and that was to buy their special clothing. Soofia needed a full-length cotton dress with enough material to cover her head as well. Karim needed two lengths of white cloth which had no joins in them. He would wrap one tightly around his waist and drape the other one over his chest and shoulders. They would wear this clothing when they got to Makkah and then they would feel at one with the other Muslims dressed in the same way.

Before they left, Karim's brother told them what one old man had told him in Makkah. 'You are travelling to the Ka'bah which is the centre of Islam . . . and you must also travel to your heart which is the centre of your life.'

Aboard the aircraft, there was a very special atmosphere. All the passengers were on hajj and many of them had waited years to be able to come and had spent their life's savings on it. All the way there, someone or other was reciting from the Qur'an and, from time to time, pilgrims would call out to Allah, 'Labbaika!' ('Here I am!') Soofia and Karim felt drawn into the mood of the hajj very deeply.

Before the plane landed at Jeddah, Soofia washed in the ritual way that she does before she says her prayers. Then she put on her special clothes. Karim did too, and so did all the other passengers: the plane was transformed!

You could not tell who was rich and who was poor, who was famous and who was unknown – nor even where anyone came from. Dressed like that, they all looked equal to each other now, just as they always are to Allah. They all had to make a special effort to be peaceful – not to fight or even quarrel, and not to harm a living thing . . .

Finally, they all arrived in Makkah. They could not keep away from the Ka'bah, even though they were hot, tired and thirsty. It was drawing them like a magnet. So they made for the Bayt-al-haram, the 'sacred house', that is, the central mosque in Makkah. The golden embroidery on the black cloth, the Kiswah, glinted in the sun. Surely, thought Soofia, the whole world was ablaze with the glory of Allah!

Then they joined the swirling crowds and moved around the Ka'bah seven times. Some people had to be carried on stretchers or chairs or even on the shoulders of friends. Soofia had never seen so many people before. . . . There were people pressing in all around her and she just let herself be carried along by this river of Muslim faith. She was part of that river now and her heart soared high. There was nothing in the world like this.

Adapted from 'Sofia and Karim go on hajj' by Angela Wood.

Task 7

1 What makes hajj more than just a trip? Working in pairs, write down five ways in which Makkah helps every Muslim feel part of the ummah, the worldwide community of Islam. Think about feelings and experiences. Sum up these ideas in five lines by using the letters of the word UMMAH.
For example:

Unbelievable experience
Makkah
Muslims together
Allah so near
Heart of Islam, my heart.

2 Think of a place that has very special meaning for you because it makes you feel part of a community, such as your family, school, group or club. Name the place and the community and then explain in a few sentences how it makes you feel about yourself. For example, your first residential trip away from your family which made you a stronger person.

● How does Jesus give a Christian identity?

When he had been with them for some time, Jesus asked his followers, 'Who do people say that I am?'

Peter, his chief disciple, answered, 'Some say you are Elijah, others say you are John the Baptist, others again say that you are a prophet.'

Jesus persisted, 'But who do you say that I am?'

'You are the MESSIAH, the son of the living God,' said Peter.

Then Jesus gave them strict orders not to tell anyone.

Luke 9.18–21.

Most of us like to know what people think about us and perhaps Jesus was no different.

Peter's first answers were not what Jesus wanted to hear. Elijah had been dead for centuries, John the Baptist was a relative. Who wanted to be just another prophet?

Peter's second answer is what Jesus was looking for. And this is what Jesus' followers still believe, whichever group (denomination) of Christians they belong to.

Christians see Jesus as their Messiah (saviour). The word Christian means follower of Jesus Christ.

But through the maze of life Christians find more in the life of Jesus. They find an example of how to live. They seek help from his teaching and example when they have to make choices in their lives. They will often turn to the first four books (the Gospels) of the New Testament for inspiration and guidance. This is where the stories of Jesus' life and teaching are found.

What would Jesus do? (WWJD)

When faced with difficult choices, Christians might ask themselves, 'What would Jesus do?' A wristband with the letters WWJD is a way of jogging their memory. This wristband also has the Christian symbol of the fish on it.

When choices have to be made, throwing a coin in the air or looking at a horoscope is not usually the best way! No, you need some criteria – some principles on which to make a decision.

Here are some examples of WWJD criteria:

1

> What you **are** as a person is more important than what you **have**.

2

> Greed for more and more money can get in the way of being happy.

3

> Don't look down on other people and forget your own failings as a person.

4

> Show care for those people who others reject.

So when you face a decision you look at your wristband and remember. It is a bit like writing a message on your hand so that you don't forget!

Task 8

1 Work in groups of four. Each look up one of the following passages in the Bible. Match yours to one of the four criteria.

- Mark 2.14–17
- Luke 18.18–25
- John 8.3–11
- Matthew 5.3–10

2 Look at the two scenarios on the right. Imagine Mark and Phoebe are into WWJD. How might this affect their behaviour or their thoughts? Which criteria might help them?

3 Invent two more scenarios where the other criteria might be useful.

4 What is your opinion of the criteria? Are they good or bad? How are they similar to or different from your own criteria for making decisions?

5 Think of a leader who has special status for you and who helps guide your decisions in the way that Jesus guides Christians. Write a paragraph about how this contributes to your identity.

Mark buys a new computer. Then he logs on to the internet and discovers there is a much faster one just launched – and it's cheaper.

Phoebe is appalled when her teacher on their school trip to France makes her share a room with Mandy who is no one's friend and gets up everyone's nose.

● How can our identity change?

Are you the same person you were at 5 hours old, 5 days, 5 weeks, 5 months, 5 years, 10 years . . . ?

Strange question, you may think: of course you are! A Buddhist would disagree.

This is an idea you may have met before. Buddhism states that everything in the universe is constantly changing; nothing stays the same. This includes human beings. Each of us is constantly changing. This change can be for the good or for the bad. **What we are and what we become is not up to anyone else but ourselves.** As we become capable of making choices and managing our thoughts, feelings and actions, we shape our own world, now and in the future.

The Buddhist 'wheel of life' sets out this idea. Buddhists call this picture the BHAVACHAKRA. 'Bhava' means becoming and 'chakra' means wheel. It is like a map or mirror of your mind showing, in symbols, the thoughts, feelings and experiences that people go through. There are four wheels in the design. Try to imagine them spinning round to show that they are not permanent, they are always changing.

Yama, the demon of death or impermanence, is shown holding up the mirror on our minds. Scary! Change can certainly frighten us.

The main part of the wheel shows different states of mind called realms. We move between these realms from moment to moment (you could experience all of them in one day) and from life to life.

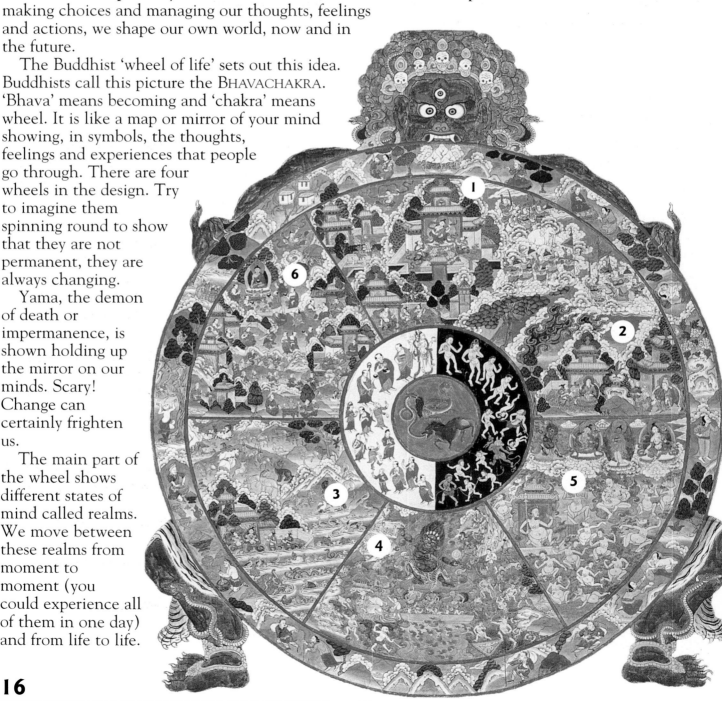

1 **Gods** A life of pleasure and contentment. But this cannot last for ever!
2 **Jealous gods or power seekers** Getting power over others, being competitive.
3 **Animals** People who just follow what they want – go with their instincts – not thinking about their actions or the consequences.
4 **Hell** People see the consequences of their evil deeds – a very aggressive realm. Can also mean times of physical and emotional suffering.
5 **Hungry ghosts** People who are so greedy they can never be satisfied.
6 **Human** The closest to the gods because humans think and choose and are capable of caring for each other.

Task 9

I Draw your own 'wheel of life' based on the six realms. Use examples that describe your own changing experiences and states of mind. These can be drawings or SYMBOLS or words. Here is the way one person described it happening in just one day:

a) Wake up hungry: animals' realm.

f) Fancy a burger and carry on eating chips, ice cream . . . until feeling sick: hungry ghosts' realm.

e) Go for a walk and look at the trees in the school grounds: gods' realm.

b) Get in a panic because it is too late to get the school bus: hell realm.

c) Find the science lesson interesting and enjoy working on paired investigation: human realm.

d) Push to the front of the dinner queue: power seekers' realm.

Wheel labels: Animal, Hell, Human, Power seekers, Gods, Hungry ghosts

2 Read again the sentence in bold in the third paragraph on page 16. It makes clear what Buddhists think about identity. In pairs, take on the role of:

A a non-Buddhist interviewer
B a Buddhist.

A prepares questions. For example, 'You could be born into a rich family – that shapes your identity, doesn't it?'
B looks up Buddhist beliefs to be sure how to answer. For example, 'You still make choices, you could lose all your money . . .'.

When you have prepared together, tape, script or role play the interview.

My identity: who am 'I'?

Who am I?

Who am I?
What am I like?
How do people see me?
Do I know myself as well as I think I do?

Who knows me best?
Who am I?
I'm a friend, a best friend
A listener

A comforter to my friends, to myself
What do I think of myself?
I'm a loner
A typical Aries, stubborn, a leader, a boss

But what about inside?
Who am I?
Going deeper, I feel
I am sensitive,

I cry to relieve what I feel inside
I'm an actor
I have split personalities
I seek attention from others

Who am I?
I love
I am loved and cared for
I'm a cousin, a niece, a granddaughter

A daughter and a child,
I always will be
A young woman, with a future ahead of me
– a husband and a family?
Who am I? Is this all?

By a Year 9 pupil.

Heroes

Heroes are funny people, dey are lost an found
Sum heroes are brainy an sum are muscle bound,
Plenty heroes die poor an are heroes after dying
Sum heroes mek yu smile when yu feel like crying.
Sum heroes are made heroes as a political trick
Sum heroes are sensible an sum are very thick!
Sum heroes are not heroes cause dey do not play de game
A hero can be young or old and have a silly name.
Drunks an sober types alike hav heroes of dere kind
Most heroes are heroes out of sight an out of mind,
Sum heroes shine a light upon a place where darkness fell
Yu could be a hero soon, yes, yu can never tell.
So if yu see a hero, better treat dem wid respect
Poets an painters say heroes are a prime subject,
Most people hav heroes even though some don't admit
I say we're all heroes if we do our little bit.

Benjamin Zephaniah.

Task 10

1 Read the poem 'Who am I?' as individual verses. Consider which verse(s) best reflects your feelings and questions and note the key ideas as points to include in your final task.
2 Who are your heroes or heroines? Why?
3 What does Benjamin Zephaniah mean in the last line? How could this affect you?

Final task

So . . . who are you?

1 Your final task is to present your own identity. How you do it is up to you. But it must reflect some of the different aspects of identity in this unit.
Here are some reminders:

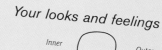

Your looks and feelings

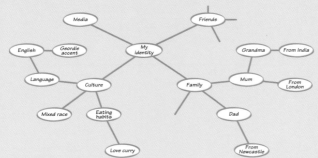

Your decisions

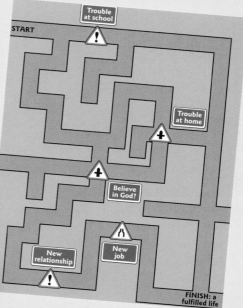

Your relationships

Your religion

2 Whatever you include, add a key to explain the most important aspects of your presentation. For example,

• what/who you consider has had the greatest effect on your identity
• what/who has had the greatest impact on the choices you have made about your direction in life.

3 'Someone with a religious faith has more purpose in life than someone who does not.'
    Do you agree/disagree with this statement? Give your opinion, with reasons. Base your answer on your own experience and the ideas in this unit.

2 From life to death: where are we going?

● The Day of the Dead

Outcomes By the end of this unit you will:

- know some similarities and differences in religious beliefs about life after death
- understand how people show what they believe through their words and actions
- evaluate these beliefs and express your own.

Literacy Summarise key ideas, sort information, analyse sacred writings, feed back to group, write a poem, make a glossary, write an essay.

Final task Write an essay comparing different religious beliefs about life after death. Look at the plan on page 37 before you start work on this unit.

In Mexico, on the first two days of November, the dead are remembered in very specific celebrations. These celebrations have complicated origins. They go far back into the history of Mexico, to ancient times and the worship of gods who were believed to control life and death. When the Spanish brought Christianity to Mexico in the sixteenth century, the priests combined the Christian All Saints' holy day with the existing traditions.

Now, the Day of the Dead combines many different religious ideas and practices and customs vary across the country. The text and pictures on the opposite page tell you about one village. But all over Mexico the day remains a very special time for thinking about death and celebrating the lives of deceased family members. It has a fun side and a serious side. The Day of the Dead ensures that death is not a taboo subject in Mexico.

● What happens on the Day of the Dead?

Preparations for the festival begin towards the end of October so that the altars at the former homes of the dead will be ready by 1 November. The altars will display images of patron saints, photographs of family members who have died, flowers, fruits, 'pan de muerto' (special bread that contains a lucky plastic skeleton toy), sugar skulls, papel picados (tissue paper patterns with skeletons) and the favourite food of the dead relative. A candle is lit for every SOUL. Then, as the sun reaches its highest point, all the souls return to town, guided by the smell of their favourite food. Souls of the children are offered toys.

It is believed that, after death, you keep your identity in order to return to the world for the 'Day of the Dead'. This is why there are so many skeletons seen at the celebrations, of all shapes and sizes, ages and occupations. Funny skeleton puppets are given to children to play with. More seriously, on the afternoon of 1 November, a coffin containing a white cardboard skeleton is carried in procession through the streets. At the house, people kneel to pray the 'Our Father'. Then they are given sugar skulls and 'pan de muerto' before holding a 'funeral' ceremony at the cemetery.

On 2 November, to the sound of the church bells, people make their way to the cemetery carrying bunches of bright flowers such as marigolds and chrysanthemums. Families sweep and wash graves and cover them with petals from their flowers. They light candles, burn incense and pray.

By midnight, all the graves are lit by hundreds of candles which shine on the faces of those who have gathered. In the sounds of whispering and sobbing, a link is renewed between those alive and their loved ones who have died.

Adapted from 'Mixquic: the Day of the Dead and the day of All Saints'.

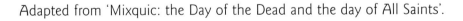

Task 1

1 Generally, in the UK, people don't like to think or talk about death. They use phrases like 'kicked the bucket' or 'passed on'. With a partner, discuss and note down reasons why it is a taboo subject. Decide how it might affect your attitudes if you were brought up in a society where the 'Day of the Dead' is part of your experience.

2 What do Mexicans believe about life after death? Write out any sentences or phrases in the text that describe their beliefs.

3 Make a table like this. In column 1, write the main activity described in each paragraph. In column 2 explain why people do this.

Activity	Meaning
Setting up an altar	Remember dead relatives

● Near–death experiences

A near-death experience describes something which people claim happened to them after they are clinically dead.

A

Mebruke *is a thirty-year-old Saudi Arabian. At the age of twenty she was swimming in the Mediterranean Sea off the coast of Italy when she became tired. As she headed for the shore, she realised she was too far out to make it back. She began to struggle and swallow water. Finally she slipped beneath the waves.*

'I went under for a fourth time, and my body went limp. I wasn't aware of it any more. It was at this point that I saw a beautiful white light. It was so bright and yet it had such a calming effect that the more I looked at it the calmer I felt. To this day I can't really say what that light was. In my religion [Islam] there are beings called angels who are made out of pure light. Maybe that is what I saw.

'Anyway, while I was underwater, I heard a voice say, "You are not to die like this". Suddenly I felt this energy shoot through me from my feet to my head, and at the same time I seemed to be propelled out of the water.

'I was moved through the water, I don't know how else to describe it. Before long a boat came, and a man reached over the side and pulled me out.'

Adapted from *Parting Visions* by Melvin Morse.

B

Beverly Brodsky *was brought up in a Jewish family in Philadelphia, USA. As a teenager, she was an* ATHEIST. *Discovering what had happened to Jews in the Holocaust had convinced her that God did not exist.*

Then, in July 1970, she had a serious motorcycle accident.

'I found myself floating on the ceiling over the bed looking down at my unconscious body. I barely had time to realise the strangeness of the situation – that I was me but not in my body – when I was joined by a radiant being bathed in a shimmering white glow. My attention was directed upward; a white light shone through – the most brilliant light I had ever seen.

'I remember travelling a long distance, very fast, upward towards the light. The entire realm seemed to be outside of time. Finally, I reached my destination. I realised I was no longer accompanied by the being who had brought me there. But I wasn't alone. There before me was the living presence of the light. I sensed intelligence, wisdom, compassion, love and truth. There was neither form nor sex to this perfect Being. Deep within me came an instant recognition: I, even I, was facing God.'

Beverly did not die. Twenty years later she said, 'I have never forgotten my heavenly voyage. Nor have I, in the face of ridicule and disbelief, ever doubted its reality. Nothing that intense and life-changing could possibly have been a dream or hallucination.'

Adapted from *Lessons from the Light* by Kenneth Ring.

What do the scientists say?

C

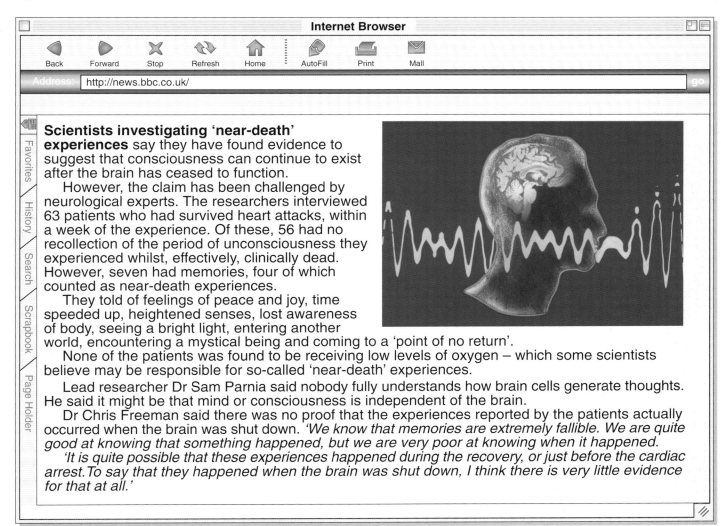

Scientists investigating 'near-death' experiences say they have found evidence to suggest that consciousness can continue to exist after the brain has ceased to function.

However, the claim has been challenged by neurological experts. The researchers interviewed 63 patients who had survived heart attacks, within a week of the experience. Of these, 56 had no recollection of the period of unconsciousness they experienced whilst, effectively, clinically dead. However, seven had memories, four of which counted as near-death experiences.

They told of feelings of peace and joy, time speeded up, heightened senses, lost awareness of body, seeing a bright light, entering another world, encountering a mystical being and coming to a 'point of no return'.

None of the patients was found to be receiving low levels of oxygen – which some scientists believe may be responsible for so-called 'near-death' experiences.

Lead researcher Dr Sam Parnia said nobody fully understands how brain cells generate thoughts. He said it might be that mind or consciousness is independent of the brain.

Dr Chris Freeman said there was no proof that the experiences reported by the patients actually occurred when the brain was shut down. *'We know that memories are extremely fallible. We are quite good at knowing that something happened, but we are very poor at knowing when it happened.*

'It is quite possible that these experiences happened during the recovery, or just before the cardiac arrest. To say that they happened when the brain was shut down, I think there is very little evidence for that at all.'

Task 2

1 Compare Sources A and B. List the things that Mebruke's and Beverly's experiences have in common.
2 With a partner, compare the stories and the research findings in Source C. Which of these points of view convinces you the most and why?

 • That these experiences are proof of an afterlife.
 • That these experiences are just the mind playing tricks on the patient.

3 Why are people interested in life after death? Write down three words or phrases. For example, 'death is a mystery'.

● **Where do you think we are going when we die?**

Is the human being just a collection of water and minerals? Does the body simply return to the earth when it dies? Or does some part of the human spirit live on?

These are big questions. Most people are interested in the answers. Religion has a lot to say about them.

Below are some points of view. Some are religious, others are not.

A The dead will be brought back to life at God's Day of JUDGEMENT sometime in the future.

B We all have a spirit or personality that I hope survives physical death. But I don't know how, what or where!

C We will go to heaven or hell. They exist. They are real.

D My soul will come back again, in another body – could be human, could be animal.

E I'm not sure but I think I believe in a life after death – maybe because I'm afraid of dying.

F There is a time of waiting between death and the Day of Judgement.

G There is absolutely nothing after death – no soul, no body, no heaven, no hell, nothing!

H There is no soul to survive – it's just that humans have a very developed brain and are big headed and emotional enough to think something of them will live on.

I The soul survives death and goes straight to a non-physical place to be with God (heaven) or without God (hell).

J This life is not the end.

K What happens to you after death depends on how you have lived this life.

Coffee in Heaven

You'll be greeted
by a nice cup of coffee
when you get to heaven
and strains of angelic harmony

But wouldn't you be devastated
if they only serve decaffeinated
while from the percolators of hell
your soul was assaulted
by SATAN's fresh espresso smell?

John Agard.

Task 3

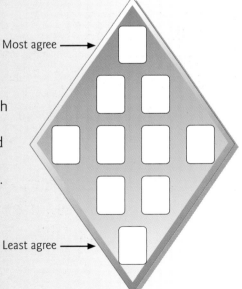

Work in pairs.

1 Write statements **A–K** on pieces of card (about 5cm by 3cm).
2 Decide if there are any other statements of your own points of view about life after death that you would like to include. Put these statements on cards too.
2 Arrange the statements in a rank order starting with the one you agree with most. You could use a diamond shape if you agree with some equally.
4 Compare your order with two other pairs. Decide which statements caused most agreement and disagreement.
5 Write a 100-word group summary and share this with the rest of the class. Start like this:

Our group agreed most with statement (A–K or your own) because ...
We disagreed most with statement (A–K) because ...
The statement we found most difficult to agree on was (A–K) because ...

Most agree →

Least agree →

6 Finally, sort the statements into categories, under the headings:

• Atheist
• Theist (if you can, say which religion)
• Agnostic.

> ATHEIST – there is no God
> THEIST – there is a God
> AGNOSTIC – uncertain

NB Some statements might fall into more than one category.

Keep this work. It's going to be important for your final task.

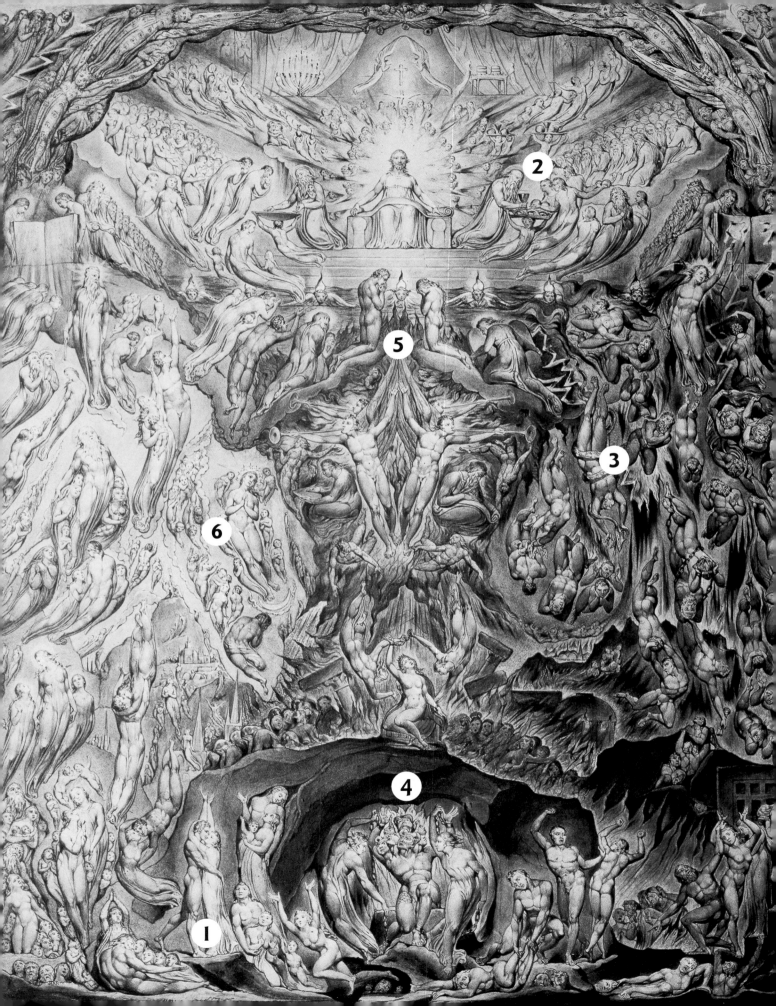

What do four religions believe about life after death?

This painting shows one artist's view of what happens after death. It is called *The Last Judgement*. It was completed in 1808 by William Blake.

1 In pairs, study the picture closely. What can you see? Discuss:
   - the small detail – what's happening at the places numbered 1–6?
   - the 'big picture' – what's the message?
2 Write down three questions you have about this painting.

'What happens to me when I die?' is one of the most crucial questions that religions try to answer. There is mystery, uncertainty and not a little fear about life after death. Some would say that this is why some people are religious – they need answers and religions provide them. But the answers are not simple. Even within the same religion, there can be differences in belief about exactly what happens.

On pages 28–35 you will find out what four of the world's religions – Hinduism, Judaism, Christianity and Islam – believe about life after death. For each religion, there will be a mixture of sources: pictures, quotations and information boxes.

Work in groups to make sure that each of the religions is covered. For example, in groups of four, each person covers one religion.

A draft report on each religion should be prepared using the same plan (see below). This report should be shared with all the group so that everyone understands some key ideas about each religion, although they may be an expert on only one!

Before you start, remind yourself of why you are going to need this in your final task – look at page 37.

Your steps to preparing a report on beliefs about life after death

1 **Read** all the information in the factfile for your chosen religion.
2 **Write** down one key belief (or more if you like) about what happens after death.
3 Find an **example** from a funeral practice that shows the belief.
4 Choose a **quote** from a sacred text that supports the belief.
5 Prepare a **glossary** of key words from the file. Use this book or another source to find their meanings and explain them in your own words.
6 **Present** your report to the rest of the group. You could read it out or word process it and give everyone a copy. Make **notes** from the other presentations.

Finally, reflect on which belief (from any religion) would most help you to cope with the death of a friend or family member.

HINDU FACTFILE

HINDU FUNERAL IN INDIA

The dead person is cremated on an open funeral pyre. The family, while sad, believe the fire is releasing the soul to take on a new form.

The ashes are traditionally scattered on water, such as at this sacred site, Pushkar Lake.

SACRED TEXTS

May you enter the shining levels as your KARMA permits.
May all that is water return to the oceans
And your body return to the soil and be one with the earth.'

Said at Hindu funerals.

As a man abandons his worn out clothes and acquires new ones, so when the body is worn out, a new one is acquired by the self, who lives within. The self cannot be pierced or burned, made wet or dry. It is everlasting and infinite, standing on the motionless foundation of eternity. It is beyond all thought, all change. Knowing this you should not grieve …

For sure is the death of all that comes to birth, sure the birth of all that dies.

From sacred writings: Bhagavad Gita 2.

From the unreal, lead me to the real, From the darkness, lead me to the light, From death, lead me to immortality.
A Hindu prayer from Brihadaranyka Upanishad I iii 28.

KEY WORDS/KEY IDEAS

REINCARNATION and release – an analogy

It is like a caterpillar climbing a tree. Think of each branch as a life.

The better the karma, the higher the climb. The worse the karma, the lower the fall – and the next incarnation.

If and when the atman (soul) reaches the top of the tree, it is released to join with Brahman – like the butterfly is released from being a caterpillar.

Key words

reincarnation	karma	atman
samsara	MOKSHA	Brahman

HINDU FUNERAL IN THE UK

Chandu Tailor & Son
FORMERLY INDIAN FUNERAL SERVICE

Ashes dispersal: some options
- *Ashes can be scattered in the Garden of Rest, witnessed by the family at the crematorium*
- *Scattering of ashes on the River Thames – a boat can be hired…*
- *River Ganges dispersal of ashes – we can help to arrange dispersal of ashes at Rishikesh on the River Ganges. Families can make their own arrangements or we are happy to disperse on your behalf during an annual pilgrimage in October/November.*

When someone dies …
- Prayers are said over the body.
- Prayers are said as the body enters the crematorium.
- The eldest son or male relative is the 'chief mourner'.
- Sacred writings are read.
- The chief mourner presses a button to make the coffin disappear. He may also ignite the cremator.
- Family and friends join together for a meal and prayers – 13 days of mourning follow.
- Traditionally, ashes are sprinkled on water – rivers, seas and especially the sacred River Ganges.

Remember to

✔ read the information
✔ find one key belief
✔ find an example of funeral practice
✔ choose a quote from a sacred text
✔ prepare a glossary
✔ present to group.

JEWISH FACTFILE

SACRED TEXTS

¹ . . .a new king will arise from David's descendants. ²The spirit of the Lord will give him wisdom, and the knowledge and skill to rule his people . . . ⁵He will rule his people with JUSTICE and integrity. ⁶Wolves and sheep will live together in peace, and leopards will lie down with young goats. Calves and lion cubs will feed together, and little children will take care of them… ⁹The land will be as full of knowledge of the Lord as the seas are full of water.

From Isaiah 11.

Today I remember with love [name], who has gone to everlasting life, and I honour his/her memory. As this light burns pure and clear, so may the thoughts of his/her goodness, shine in my heart and strengthen me, Lord, to do your will. Amen.

Kaddish prayer said at a person's funeral and on each anniversary of their death. A candle is lit as the prayer is said.

A Jewish poem reflecting on the greatness of God and the frailty of human life

¹ O Lord, you have always been our home.
² Before you created the hills or brought the world into being,
you were eternally God, and will be God for ever.
³ You tell man to return to what he was;
you change him back to dust.
⁴ A thousand years to you are like one day;
they are like yesterday, already gone,
like a short hour in the night.
⁵ You carry us away like a flood;
we last no longer than a dream.
We are like weeds that sprout in the morning,
⁶ that grow and burst into bloom,
then dry up and die in the evening
¹² Teach us how short our life is,
so that we may become wise.

From Psalm 90.

KEY WORDS/KEY IDEAS

Two views on RESURRECTION

1 I believe with perfect faith that there will be a resurrection of the dead at a time when it will please the Creator, blessed be his name, and exalted be the remembrance of him for ever and ever.

This is one of the thirteen basic beliefs of Jews written by a twelfth-century Jewish teacher called Maimonides. His ideas are still very important to Jews today.

2 Resurrection of the dead does not necessarily imply identity with the material composing the body when alive; rather that the sum total of all our deeds and thoughts, habits and character, does not vanish into nought at the moment of death. There is for the soul in the world-to-come identity of personality with the soul in the earthly life.

Rabbi J H Hertz, from a commentary on the prayer book.

Key words

Kaddish   BET CHAYIM   soul

resurrection   Reform

Orthodox   shiva

A JEWISH FUNERAL

When someone dies ...

- The body is wrapped in a simple cloth, often the tallit or prayer shawl for a man.
- The bereaved make a small tear in their clothing as a symbol of their grief.
- Prayers are said at a short service.
- Mourners throw earth on the coffin, which may be made of biodegradable wood and rope handles to represent that nothing physical lasts for ever.
- The Kaddish prayer is said.
- ORTHODOX Jews will bury their dead in simple graves; Reform Jews are not opposed to cremation.
- For seven days, mourners will stay with the bereaved to comfort them. This time is called SHIVA.

Remember to

✔ read the information
✔ find one key belief
✔ find an example of funeral practice
✔ choose a quote from a sacred text
✔ prepare a glossary
✔ present to group.

31

CHRISTIAN FACTFILE

SACRED TEXTS

Words of Jesus used at many Christian funerals:

I am the resurrection and the life. Whoever believes in me will live, even though he dies; and whoever lives and believes in me will never die.

John 11.25–26.

There are many rooms in my Father's house, and I am going to prepare a place for you.

John 14.2.

A vision of hope

Then I saw a new heaven and a new Earth . . .

Now God's home is with mankind! He will live with them, and they shall be his people. God himself will be with them, and He will be their God. He will wipe away all tears from their eyes. There will be no more death, no more grief or crying or pain. The old things have disappeared.

Revelation 21.1–4.

We believe in the resurrection of the body and the life everlasting

From the Apostles' Creed – a statement of Christian belief recited in many churches.

A CHRISTIAN FUNERAL

When someone dies . . .

- Many churches hold a special service including hymns, prayers, Bible readings and, sometimes, a EUCHARIST.
- The dead person may be buried or cremated.
- At a burial, earth will be thrown on the coffin; at a cremation, special words will be said as the coffin disappears from view. In both cases, the words are similar – including the phrase 'earth to earth, ashes to ashes'.
- Traditionally, black is worn.

Remember to

✔ read the information
✔ find one key belief
✔ find an example of funeral practice
✔ choose a quote from a sacred text
✔ prepare a glossary
✔ present to group.

Christian views on the Day of Judgement

> I believe in the traditional teaching of my church [Roman Catholic] When we die, we go to heaven if we have repented of our sins. If we have sinned and not repented then we go to PURGATORY to be made fit for heaven. Those who refuse to believe or repent will go to hell. Finally, Jesus will come back to Earth. The dead will be resurrected and all those souls will be reunited with their bodies. God will judge everyone. There will be a new heaven and a new Earth. The resurrected from heaven will live there for ever. The resurrected from hell will return there for ever.

> At some point in the future, known only to God, everyone will be judged. If you believe that Jesus died for your sins and you have tried to live by his teachings then you will go to heaven. If not, you will go to hell. Those who have died already will be included in the judgement at that time.

> I am not sure that there will be a physical Day of Judgement. I think you make your own heaven and hell on earth when you accept God or reject God.

Christian views on heaven and hell

> Heaven is an actual place. It will be wonderful there because you are with God and there is total happiness and peace.

> Heaven is SPIRITUAL not physical. The body dies but the soul lives on. It is like a state of being totally at peace because you are in the presence of God.

> Hell is an actual place where there is only sorrow and suffering.

> Hell is being separated from God – it means your soul is always suffering and sad.

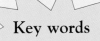

Key words

heaven   hell

Day of Judgement

resurrection   eternal life

KEY WORDS/KEY IDEAS

Angels in a heavenly landscape by Benozzo di Gozzoli. A physical heaven that looks much like Earth.

MUSLIM FACTFILE

Muslim views of heaven and hell

Angels from
*The Wonders of
Creation*, Iraq, 1280

The Vision of Hell,
Turkey, 1583

Muhammad's Paradise, Persia, 1030

Main beliefs

This life is a preparation and a test for life after death.	At some point in the future, Allah will bring the world to an end, the dead will be raised and everyone will be judged.	Eternal life (AKHIRAH) will begin and go on for ever.

For those who have already died, there is a time of waiting (BARZAKH).

You will be judged on how you have lived as a Muslim, following Allah's teaching in the Qur'an and the Islamic law (SHARI'AH).

A record is kept of your behaviour. If your good deeds outweigh your bad, then you will go to paradise; if your bad deeds outweigh your good, then you will go to hell. Even your intentions are counted.

After burial, Muslims believe two angels question the dead person to find out if they are fit to enter paradise.

SACRED TEXTS/KEY WORDS

Paradise

His shall be a blissful state in a lofty garden, with clusters of fruit within his reach. We shall say to him, 'Eat and drink to your heart's content: your reward for what you did in days gone by.'

Qu'ran (Surah 69.19).

It is Allah who gives you life, then gives you death, then he will gather you together for the Day of Judgement.

Qur'an (Surah 45.26).

Hell

Garments of fire have been prepared for the unbelievers. Scalding water shall be poured upon their heads, melting their skins and that which is in their bellies. They shall be lashed with rods of iron.

Qu'ran (Surah 22.19).

Key words

Akhirah   paradise   hell

Qur'an   Barzakh   Shari'ah

A MUSLIM FUNERAL

When someone dies . . .
- The body is washed by someone of the same sex, or by the husband or wife.
- The body is wrapped in simple white robes – if the person has been on the annual pilgrimage, their pilgrimage robe will be used.
- A funeral prayer is recited over the body.
- Muslims always bury the body; cremation is not practised.
- Handfuls of earth are dropped into the grave as the body is placed in it.
- In Muslim countries, the body is buried without a coffin and with the head and right side facing Mecca.

Remember to

- ✔ read the information
- ✔ find one key belief
- ✔ find an example of funeral practice
- ✔ choose a quote from a sacred text
- ✔ prepare a glossary
- ✔ present to group.

● Two very different views on death

A

TURN YOUR BEST FRIEND INTO A DIAMOND!

Diamonds may be a girl's best friend, but now you can turn your best friend into a diamond.

A company in Chicago claims that it has developed a process for turning cremated human remains into diamonds that can be worn as jewellery.

'We're building on the simple fact that all living creatures are carbon-based and diamonds are carbon-based,' said [the] head of LifeGem Memorials, which has begun marketing the . . . diamonds as the answer for people who think a headstone or an urn . . . is too impersonal.

The Times.

B

This poem was written by someone who was dying. It is part of an anthology of poetry written by people being cared for in a hospice.

All partings come
unexpected or expected
if in one or a hundred years;
but those unavowed links of love
are not broken
so true are the words we have spoken:
Eternity is ours, and, unwelcome death,
know this now
For us you hold no fears.

'Know this now' by Grace Smith,
from *Travellers' Tales.*

Task 6

1 Which religions would think of this diamond technology as:
   a) up to the individual to decide?
   b) against their teaching?
   Give reasons for your answers.
2 a) In what ways is 'Know this now' a religious poem?
   b) Could it be used by a non-religious person? Why?
   c) What is **your** reaction to the poem?

Task 7

Before you start your final task, do this as a group.

On page 24 there were eleven different opinions expressed about life after death and you also added some of your own. Complete this chart. For each opinion decide which religion agrees and tick the column. If people hold different views within the same religion, you will need to add 'some' in the column.

Quotation	Hindu	Jew	Christian	Muslim
a) The dead will be brought back.		✓ (some)	✓	✓

Looking back

In this unit, you have looked at:

- Is death something to celebrate?
- Near-death experiences
- Where do you think we are going when we die?
- What do four religions believe about life after death?

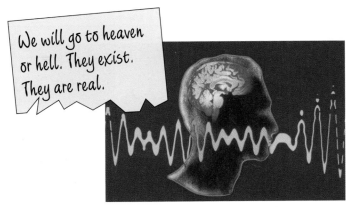

We will go to heaven or hell. They exist. They are real.

Final task

So . . . where are we going?

1 You are going to write an essay with the title 'Life after death: what lies beyond the grave?' Your aim is to explain what religions say about life after death and to explain your own views. You can use this structure:

Introduction   What the title means. Why do some people believe in life after death and others not?

Paragraph One   Give some examples of how people respond to the puzzle and mystery of death, for example the Mexican Day of the Dead. Any suggestions from your own or others' experience?

Paragraph Two   Similarities between religions: check your notes and Task 8. Find at least two things that are *similar* in all religions. These could be beliefs or things people do.

Paragraph Three   Differences between religions: check your notes and Task 8. Find at least two examples of *differences* between religions. Again, these could be beliefs or actions.

Paragraph Four   Differences within one religion: identify where people from within the *same* religion hold *different* opinions. Check Task 8 again.

Conclusion   Give your own opinion on the key question. Which ideas have **you** found convincing and which unconvincing?

Then if you wish:

2 Write a poem to express your own thoughts, feelings, hopes and fears about life after death. Include interesting ideas from your essay. Look back at the second parts of Tasks 6 and 7 for help.

Why is it sometimes hard to believe in God?

This unit is an introduction to Units 4–6. It sets the scene and helps you begin planning for a class debate on reasons to believe or not to believe in God. The debate cannot take place unless you have studied some, if not all, of these units.

Internet Browser

Back   Forward   Stop   Refresh   Home   AutoFill   Print   Mall

Address: http://www.bbc.co.uk/newsround   go

Favorites | History | Search | Scr

Thousands choose Star Wars as a 'religion'

Star Wars fans have made Jedi the fourth most popular 'religion' in England and Wales.

Every ten years, a census counts everyone in Britain and asks questions about their country of birth, their ethnic group and their religion. In the 2001 census, people were asked what faith they believed in.

There had been an internet rumour that if enough people put down that they believed in Jedi, it would be classed officially as a religion. It didn't work because the Office for National Statistics counted them as people who did not believe in God. But 390,000 (0.7 per cent of the population of England and Wales) voted for Jedi, making it the fourth most popular choice after Christianity, Islam and Hinduism!

Outcomes By the end of this unit you will:

- explain some religious beliefs about God
- give your own initial opinions on issues that create problems for belief in God
- know and be able to use key words and their meanings.

Literacy Research, survey and evaluate results, write a description, write a summary, give a personal response.

Final task Complete a pyramid summarising the main points in this unit, drawing together all your thoughts on the key question.

● Why choose Jedi as a religion?

Star Wars is a hugely successful series of films or 'episodes' that began in the 1970s. It has a massive following.

But why claim Jedi as a religion? Were people just trying to confuse the census results? Were they serious about Jedi being a religion?

The series is about the struggle between good and evil 'long, long ago, in a galaxy far, far away'. The Jedi knights are the force for good, the guardians of peace and justice in the galaxy. Obi Wan Kenobi (opposite) is an important Jedi knight who was one of the few to survive an attack by corrupt leaders. These leaders were served by Darth Vader, a Jedi knight who gave in to the dark force and used his training for evil purposes. The 'force' (symbolised by the light sabre), which could have achieved so much good, was manipulated by him and so evil ruled in the galaxy. Stormtroopers carried out a reign of terror until the evil Emperor was defeated and the Rebel Alliance of freedom fighters restored peace.

What about the other 99.3 per cent of the population?

What other religions did people choose?

The census asked, 'Do you have a faith? If yes, state which'. The table shows you what the other 99.3 per cent of the population chose.

Religion	Number of followers (England and Wales)	Percentage
Christian	37,338,486	71.7
Muslim	1,546,626	3.0
Hindu	552,421	1.1
Sikh	329,358	0.6
Jewish	259,927	0.5
Buddhist	144,453	0.3
Other religions	150,720	0.3
No religion	7,709,267	14.8
Chose not to answer that question	4,010,658	7.7
Total	52,041,916	100

Task 1

1 Discuss: The Jedi followers were included under 'no religion'. Do you think that is fair? Give reasons.

2 a) Using your numeracy skills, choose a way to show the data in the table, such as a graph or a chart.

   b) Summarise what the information tells you about the present state of religious belief in England and Wales.

   • What proportion of people say they are religious?
   • What proportion believe in God (remember most Buddhists do not believe in God)?

3 Research the same information with your class/year group/ school/parents/friends. Ask the same question of 20 people and tabulate the results. Use ICT to set out your survey, its findings and your evaluation.

● God is . . .

Here are some ways that different people (religious and non-religious) would finish the sentence 'God is . . .'.

...Creator
...LAW GIVER
...Father, Son and Holy Spirit
...all knowing
truth
God is...
...judge
...almighty
...heard through the prophets
...indescribable

Task 2

Write each word or phrase on a separate slip of paper. Working with a partner, you are going to arrange these words in different ways.

1 Sort them into those which suggest the speakers believe in God (theists), the speakers don't believe in God (atheists), the speakers are not sure (agnostics).
2 Group them into pairs or trios that are **similar**: for example 'present in all life' and 'in us'.
3 Find pairs that are **opposites**. For example: 'far above us' and 'all around us'.
4 Arrange the words as a wordscape, adding words or phrases of your own if you wish to show your own ideas about God. A wordscape is when you use words or phrases to make a picture or design.
5 Below are some questions that could be asked about God. Add to them. Give more examples. Work out questions you would like answered.

...One
...everlasting
...everywhere

If God is . . .	then why . . .?
everywhere	can't I see . . .?
almighty	not use power in the world to prevent . . .?

...irrelevant

...above all things

...the Greatest

...outside time

...Lord

...Judge

...unique

God is...

...fearless

...SEEN IN JESUS

...a myth

...present in all life

...found along many different paths

...far above us

...in us

...peace

...all around us

...a mystery

● What makes it hard to believe in God?

Units 4–6 examine three issues that can make it hard for some people to believe in God. This spread is an introduction to these three issues.

Issue 1

Science

Some people say science has disproved religion and has ditched God.
(Unit 4)

Issue 2

Suffering

Some people say that the amount of suffering in the world proves that God does not exist.
(Unit 5)

Issue 3

Evil

Some people say that the power of evil proves that God does not exist
(Unit 6).

*It might indeed be comforting to believe in a god, but **just because something is comforting doesn't make it true**. Truth means scientific truth.*
Dr Richard Dawkins.

I believe in God, despite the absence of positive proof. My faith provides me with a purpose [for the universe] . . . I find science a fascinating subject but rather cold and impersonal.
Professor Sir Arnold Wolfendale.

These two scientists have different beliefs about God and science. Which view do you support at this stage?

Where is he?

I'd like to see God.
I'd like to tell him a few things.
I'd like to say:
'God, why do you create people
and make them suffer *and fight in vain,*
and live brief unhappy lives like pigs,
and make them die disgustingly,
and rot?

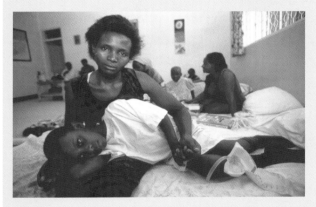

That's what I'd say to God
if I could find him hiding behind a tree.
But God's a wise guy.
He keeps in hiding!

Anonymous poem.

Is God to blame for suffering? Or is God helpless to prevent suffering? Which makes more sense to you at this stage?

These words were broadcast from Ely Cathedral during a service to celebrate the lives of two murdered schoolgirls, Holly Wells and Jessica Chapman, from Soham in Cambridgeshire. The vicar's message to the millions listening was:

'We need to let our lives be ruled by love and goodness, not ruled by hate and the deeds of darkness . . . The witness of the many flowers . . . the huge numbers of cards testify . . . to the power of love and goodness. They show ultimately that **the power of love is far stronger, than the works of wickedness**. *The darkness may seem to win for a while, but in the end light and goodness will prevail.'*

Ian Huntley's house, where the girls died, is demolished, April 2004.

Is good more powerful than evil? What do you think at this stage?

Task 3

1 Discuss each of the three key issues on this spread. Use the questions to start you talking.
2 Now focus on the four statements in **bold**. Decide how strongly you agree or disagree with each one on a scale of 1–10 (1 = total agreement with the statement; 10 = total disagreement). You could do this as an 'opinion line', placing your Post-It somewhere between 1 and 10 on a line across a desk or across a classroom.
    You must be prepared to say **why** you have placed yourself in this position!

● Teenage voices

The problem I have is the absence of real proof. If you can't prove something, how do you know it's true?

Ann, 13

I am tempted to believe because I see God working through good religious people who help the poor, but then I see non-religious people doing that, so I don't know what to believe!

Denzil, 14

There is something about us that is spiritual. But that doesn't mean there is a God. It just means that we have highly developed brains. Religion is like an insurance policy – people believe in God, just in case there is one!

Kirsty, 15

I've always believed in God – my family do. I do think about it even though I don't go to church. There must be something more to life than getting from birth to death with as much success and happiness as possible.

Neela, 13

He does not exist. He is a figment of the human imagination thought up to provide a role model for humanity, that is why he is made up entirely of perfect human traits. God is central to religion and religion is the opium of the people.

James, 16

I believe there is only one God but he has many names and forms. He never had a beginning and will never have an end. He is the creator of all, everything was formed from him and at the end of this time everything will return to him.

John, 15

There are not enough words to describe God: omniscient, omnipotent and omnipresent spring to mind, however they do not begin to touch on the boundaries of God's awesomeness. He created the world out of nothingness. He personally knows and understands each being individually (whether they wish to know Him or not). God is totally without parallel – no number of earthly descriptions can come close to creating an image of Him. The only way to know what he is like is to experience Him.

Shelley, 16

Task 4

1 Write a short **anonymous** statement, summarising your personal belief/opinion on whether God exists. You can **either** use/adapt one of the views opposite **or** write your own. The important thing is that this is **your** view. But make sure it remains anonymous: word-process it if you can.
2 Put all the statements in a box and take turns to pick one and read it out.
3 Discuss the statements in small groups.
   You may then wish to revise your own statement in the light of these discussions – do so now before you do the final task.
4 Create a class display of statements. This will be a reference throughout your investigation of Units 4–6.

Final task

So . . . why is it sometimes hard to believe in God?

Your debate on page 91 must be built on firm foundations of knowledge and understanding. You are now going to summarise the main points of your learning in this introductory unit. This pyramid diagram should help you. Each layer summarises one spread from the unit. It should be a setting out of what you know, what you believe, the questions you would like answers to, and so on. It should be useful throughout Units 4–6 and in the final debate.

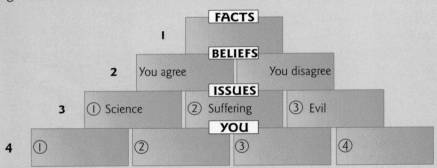

Layer 1 (see pages 38–39)
The place of religion and belief in God in the UK.
The overall views of your class/school/year/family/friends.

Layer 2 (see pages 40–41)
Beliefs about God.
In the left box write two statements about God with which you **agree**.
In the right box write two statements about God with which you **disagree**.

Layer 3 (see pages 42–43)
Summarise your personal response to one (or more) of the issues.

Layer 4 (see page 44)
List four things – your questions, your puzzles, your concerns, your beliefs – about God.

Remember to refer back to this summary when the class holds its debate.

walking in space

● It makes you think...

This extract is taken from *Letters from Mir* by Jerry M. Linenger, an American astronaut. He wrote to his son while in space in 1997.

Dear John,

. . . As far as my space walk felt, imagine this. You are in scuba gear. Your vision is restricted by the size of your underwater mask. Your fins, wetsuit and gloves make you clumsy and bulky. The water is . . . thickly frozen overhead with only one entry–exit hole drilled into the ice. Your life depends on your gear functioning properly the entire time. The farther away you venture, the farther away you are from the re-entry hole drilled in the ice . . .

You are not in water, but on a cliff. Crawling, slithering, gripping, reaching. You are not falling from the cliff; instead the whole cliff is falling and you are on it . . . When you look down you see no bottom. You just fall and fall and fall.

The sun sets swiftly. Blackness totally envelops you. The darkness is not merely dark, but absolute black. You see nothing, nothing.

Your eyes finally adjust to the darkness and you can begin to make out forms. Another human, your space-walking partner, is being silhouetted against the heavens. When it first became dark, you were falling feet first. Now, five minutes later, as the cliff – which is the space station itself – rotates, you feel as if you have reached the crest of a roller coaster and are now barrelling down steeply. So steeply that you have the sensation of falling headfirst out of your seat and toward Earth. . . . You rationally know that you are still attached to the space station and that the station, not yourself, has rotated. But you feel differently, you feel upside-down. You want to flip back upright, but you cannot mentally make it happen. You finally convince yourself that it is okay to be diving headfirst into nothing . . .

. . . Good night, John. I hope that you are not awakened by a nightmare where you are falling, falling. The space shuttle will be coming soon to pick me up. It is downhill from there.

Love,

Dad

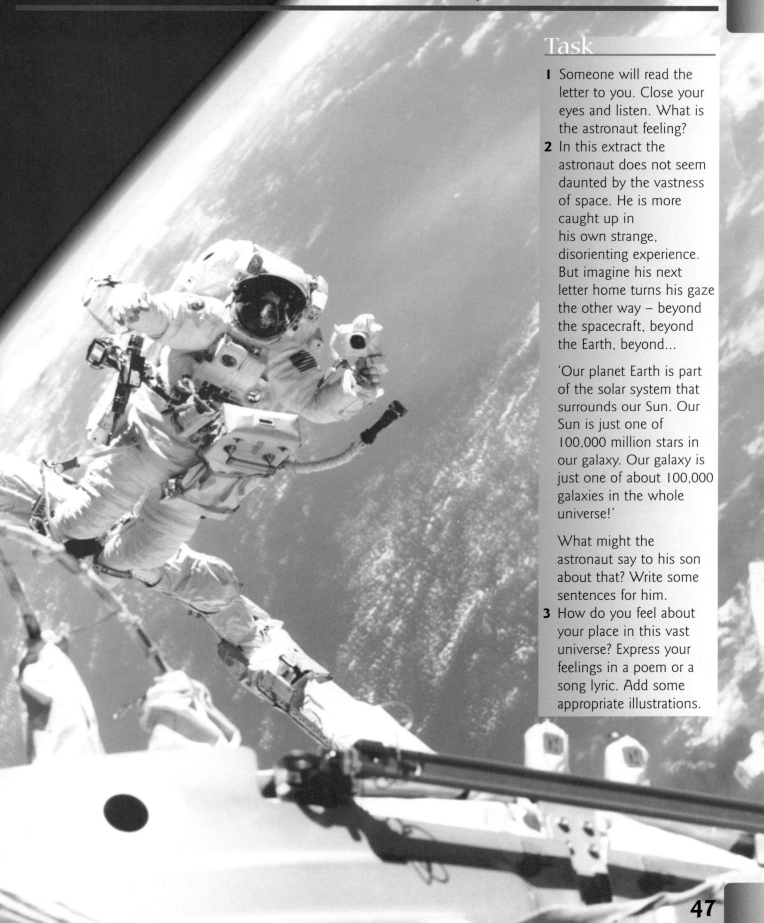

Task

1 Someone will read the letter to you. Close your eyes and listen. What is the astronaut feeling?

2 In this extract the astronaut does not seem daunted by the vastness of space. He is more caught up in his own strange, disorienting experience. But imagine his next letter home turns his gaze the other way – beyond the spacecraft, beyond the Earth, beyond...

'Our planet Earth is part of the solar system that surrounds our Sun. Our Sun is just one of 100,000 million stars in our galaxy. Our galaxy is just one of about 100,000 galaxies in the whole universe!'

What might the astronaut say to his son about that? Write some sentences for him.

3 How do you feel about your place in this vast universe? Express your feelings in a poem or a song lyric. Add some appropriate illustrations.

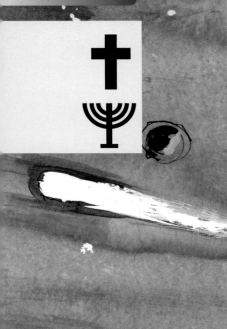

● How it all began: a scientific story

In the beginning . . . or was there a beginning? Some people think the universe did not begin because it is full of energy that never stops. This energy goes through cycles, which means that the universe is continually expanding and contracting and then expanding again. Others think that the universe began with a 'big bang'. But all of these people agree that the universe is always changing.

Over 12 billion years ago the universe was a mass of vast, hot, swirling clouds of gas. Planets, galaxies, suns and stars were formed as the gases cooled. Countless millions of stars were made.

Our own galaxy, the Milky Way, was made like this. It has millions of stars.

Our sun is one, out towards the edge of the galaxy. Many gases swirled around the sun as it began to form. From these gases, the earth and all the other planets in the solar system were made. This happened over four and a half thousand million years ago.

The ultra-violet light from the sun, along with electricity from thunderstorms and great heat from the violently erupting volcanoes on earth, caused the gases and waters to produce the earliest forms of life. For millions of years, these single cells slowly developed. They formed many-celled things, then more complicated living things. So began the journey of life which is called EVOLUTION.

New living things appeared because of changes which the earth went through, because of changes in the cells themselves. Those which fitted in best with their surroundings were the most likely to live and give birth to the next generation.

Outcomes By the end of this unit you will:

- explain some different religious and scientific points of view about the origins of the universe
- give an informed opinion about whether or not science and religion are in conflict
- evaluate the importance of humans in CREATION.

Literacy Analyse a story, discuss in groups, write a summary and comparison, make a concept map of key points.

Final task Draw a concept map to show how science and religion agree and disagree and then analyse it.

Life spread from the waters on to the land and then into the air. Some creatures, like the dinosaurs, died out. Some appear to have remained unchanged for millions of years. Others have evolved to give the present amazing range of living creatures.

So, over the years, different forms of life have evolved. We humans, along with the apes, have evolved from a common ancestor. But now humans have powers which can either improve or destroy the world. This means that the future of the world depends on what we choose to do.

From *Worlds of Difference* by Martin Palmer and Esther Bisset.

Task 1

Here is a grid for you to complete. On a copy of it, fill in the first column from this spread. Do the second column from pages 50–51.

Questions	Science story	Genesis story
Who/what is in control?		
Process? **a)** Timescale		
b) Sequence		
Importance of humans?		
Universe – accident or plan?		

● **How it all began: a religious story**

There are many religious stories about the creation of the universe. For example, in Hinduism, many universes are created and destroyed. The creation story in Islam has many features in common with those in Judaism and Christianity.

In the beginning, when God created the universe, the earth was formless and desolate. The raging ocean that covered everything was engulfed in total darkness, and the spirit of God was moving over the water. Then God commanded, 'Let there be light' – and light appeared. God was pleased with what he saw. Then he separated the light from the darkness and he named the light 'Day' and the darkness 'Night'. Evening passed and morning came – that was the first day.

Then God commanded, 'Let there be a dome to divide the water and to keep it in two separate places' – and it was done. So God made a dome, and it separated the water under it from the water above it. He named the dome 'Sky'. Evening passed and morning came – that was the second day.

Then God commanded, 'Let the water below the sky come together in one place, so that land will appear' – and it was done. He named the land, 'Earth', and the water which had come together he named 'Sea'. And God was pleased with what he saw. Then he commanded, 'Let the earth produce all kinds of plants, those that bear grain and those that bear fruit' – and it was done. So the earth produced all kinds of plants, and God was pleased with what he saw. Evening passed and morning came – that was the third day.

Then God commanded, 'Let lights appear in the sky to separate day from night and to show the times when days, years and seasons begin; they will shine in the sky to give light to the earth' – and it was done. So God made the two larger lights, the sun to rule over the day and the moon to rule over the night; he also made the stars. He placed the lights in the sky to shine on the earth, to rule over the day and the night, and to separate light from darkness. And God was pleased with what he saw. Evening passed and morning came – that was the fourth day.

Then God commanded, 'Let the water be filled with many kinds of living creatures, and let the air be filled with birds.' So God created the great sea monsters, all kinds of creatures that live in the water, and all kinds of birds. And God was pleased with what he saw. He blessed them and told the creatures that live in the waters to reproduce, and to fill the sea, and he told the birds to increase in number. Evening passed and morning came – that was the fifth day.

Then God commanded, 'Let the earth produce all kinds of animal life: domestic and wild, large and small' – and it was done. So God made them all, and he was pleased with what he saw.

Then God said, 'And now we will make human beings; they will be like us and resemble us. They will have power over the fish, the birds and all the animals, domestic and wild, large and small.' So God created human beings, making them to be like himself. He created them male and female, blessed them and said, 'Have many children, so that your descendants will live all over the earth and bring it under their control. I am putting you in charge of the fish, the birds and all the wild animals. I have provided all kinds of grain and all kinds of fruit for you to eat; but for all the wild animals and all the birds I have provided grass and leafy plants for food' – and it was done. God looked at everything he had made, and he was very pleased. Evening passed and morning came – that was the sixth day.

And so the whole universe was completed. By the seventh day, God had finished what he had been doing and stopped working. He blessed the seventh day and set it apart as a special day, because by that day he had completed his creation and stopped working. And that is how the universe was created.

Genesis 1–2.14.

Task 2

1 Identify and list the similarities and differences between the two 'stories'. You could use the questions from the chart as categories.

2 Now focus on just one question: **How did the universe begin?** Discuss in groups:
  a) What is the most important difference between the two accounts?
  b) What is the most important similarity between the two accounts?
  c) Could they both be true?

3 For your final task you are going to be preparing a concept map recording and connecting key ideas in this unit. You may have prepared concept maps before but, in case not, here are the most important rules:

• Use a large sheet of paper so you have lots of room.
• Use lots of different colours.
• Use as few words as possible – only the words you will need to understand what you have written.
• Use pictures as well – with the words or instead of words.

The sources cover lots of things but you are going to focus on just the origins of the universe. Here are the beginnings. Use your completed table from page 49 and the two sources on pages 48–51 to add to it. Remember, a concept map is **your way of looking at things**. Your map doesn't have to look like the example here.

You need to know

Some Jews and Christians believe this story to be factually correct – the world was created in six days. They believe that the Bible is literally true, that God is 'big' enough for this.

Some say that each day in the story represents a period of time. The Genesis story can be matched to the scientific story in the sequence set out in both. God created the universe and scientists are only now beginning to find out how.

Others believe that the truth of the story is in its meaning. It is a religious MYTH – a story to explain a mystery and to teach a belief. Scientific and historical discoveries and theories are welcome as they reveal more and more about the wonders of God's universe.

● What did God have to do with it?

Almost everyone in the worlds of science and religion would agree that the universe is an amazing place. Where they might disagree is **why** it is so amazing. Is it because God planned it this way or did it just happen?

A

Nobody would look at a watch and believe that it came into being as a result of an accident. It is far too complex. It has to have a designer. So it is with the universe. It is incredibly complex, in every detail – from the tiniest molecule to the furthest planet. There has to be a designer. It could never have evolved to that degree of accuracy by accident alone.

B

The Big Bang was pure chance. How can we possibly know that our ideas about cause and effect operated billions of years ago? There is no need to invent a cause – it just happened.

C

There is evidence that our part of the universe, the Earth, has weaknesses in its design. The number of NATURAL DISASTERS that occur regularly – earthquakes, droughts, floods – point to an imperfect design. Or to no design, or designer, at all.

D

Something cannot come out of nothing. Everything that happens has a cause of some sort. So, for the universe to exist at all, there must be a reason or cause, and that 'cause' must be God.

E

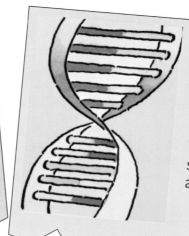

God had a plan for the universe which led to human beings. We are all unique, for example we all have different fingerprints and DNA. This uniqueness is surely not just an accident!

F

Darwin's THEORY of evolution explains why living things are as they are. Life was very simple to begin with but became more and more complicated as species adapted to the changing circumstances of their environment. This was more by the survival of the fittest than by any plan or design. Human beings have more developed brains – that's all.

Task 3

1 Read statements **A–F**. Which of these suggest that the universe was the result of God's plan? Which suggest the universe was the result of an accident?
2 Which viewpoint do you find most convincing? Why?
3 Write an acrostic poem expressing your view: 'Accident or Plan'. You could use the word UNIVERSE. For example, two people who believed in 'Accident' or 'Plan' could start like this:

Uncontrolled	**U**nbelievable but
No plan	**N**ot
Immense	**I**mpossible
V	**V**
E	**E**
R	**R**
S	**S**
E	**E**

4 Now return to your Origins of the Universe mini-concept map. This spread should give you lots to add to it.

● Are human beings special?

The human being is perhaps the most amazing of all 'creations'. For example:

A British scientist has calculated that, over an 80-year life span, 'the human brain processes 10 terabytes of data, equivalent to the storage capacity of 7,142,857,142,860, 000 floppy disks'.
'Death has had its chips',
Daily Telegraph.

And we still do not know everything! But does this mean that human beings are special to God? Does having a better brain than other animals make us special?

And what about feelings? Do they make us special? We may think that we are in love but some say that how we go about choosing partners can be reduced to gene and hormone science. We are just looking for the best mate to ensure our species continues – just like any other animal!

However a common religious view is that human beings are different from animals. It can be summed up like this:

Human beings are made in God's image – there is a little bit of God in us. Humans have a soul.
They have a special relationship with God – and God wants us to develop that relationship.
God has a plan for each person – it is the individual's role to find that plan and live according to that plan.
Humans have a higher consciousness than animals – able to make moral choices, able to tell the difference between right and wrong.

This is a central part of the Genesis account of creation on pages 50–51. Even religious people who do not accept that the story of Genesis is literally true still accept the part about humans having a special relationship with God.

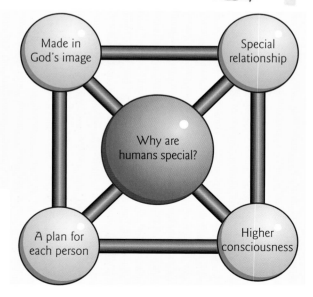

So...

A Are humans 'special'? Are they the pinnacle of creation, the outcome of an amazing evolutionary process, with the capacity to have a special relationship with God?

or...

B Are humans just the present outcome of that process of evolution, with nothing more than a very sophisticated brain?

The sources below express different opinions.

G

To teach children that they are nothing more than developed mutations who evolved from something akin to a monkey, and that death is the end of everything, is hardly going to [fill] them with a sense of purpose, self-worth and respect.

Headteacher of a Christian school.

H

Natural selection, the blind, unconscious, automatic process which Darwin discovered, and which we now know is the explanation for the existence and apparently purposeful form of all life, has no purpose in mind . . . It has no mind . . . It does not plan for the future.

Dr Richard Dawkins, zoologist.

Task 4

1 In groups, discuss the quotations (**G** and **H**).
2 Agree a group response to the question,
'Are human beings special ?'
Some/most of us agree because................................
Some/most of us disagree because............................
So the majority believe human beings are/are not special.
3 a) How will humans evolve? On a large sheet of paper, draw a diagram like this. Fill it in to show your ideas.

- What will happen to the natural world – and how will human beings respond?
- What will happen to the global population? Will inequalities be solved or strengthened?
- What will be the advances in medical science? No more disease? More powerful viruses?
- Where will we live? In space? Or beneath the sea?

b) Write a conclusion to your drawing stating if you think life will get better or worse for the human race. State reasons why you see the future as you do. What difference does it make if humans **are** special (A, above) or if they **aren't** (B)?

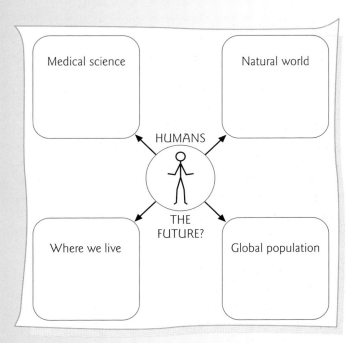

● Can faith heal?

In recent years, there have been claims that there is a strong link between health and spirituality. Medical science is taking an interest. Why?

What is meant by spirituality?

Spirituality is not just about organised religion. It is the belief that humans have a spirit, some would call it a soul. There is something more to being human than just the cells of a body. Most would agree that a very healthy body does not guarantee a very happy, contented person! Both religious and non-religious people recognise a spiritual aspect to human identity.

What is the evidence that religion has a positive effect on health?

For religious people, spirituality is to do with God or a belief in a power greater than themselves. So for them, prayer is crucial to their well-being. But does it make a difference?

There are cases where, despite prayer and faith, the person dies. So, where is God then?

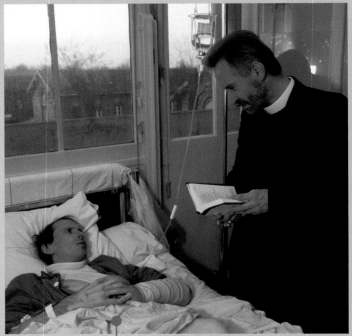

A hospital chaplain visiting a patient.

> What sort of God heals one person and not another?

> God can do more than we can ask or think!

Research studies into religion and health

- A study of 21,000 people from 1987 to 1995 found that those who attended religious services more than once a week lived, on average, seven years longer than those who never attended.
- Psychologists from Sheffield University found that people who pray more have lower levels of depression and anxiety.

But religious people may be more likely to avoid damaging habits such as smoking and drinking. Also they will probably have the support of a community.

Research is being carried out in Scotland into how to help patients' spiritual as well as medical needs. Some medical schools in the UK are teaching future doctors about the importance of understanding both these needs in helping their patients.

In a Birmingham hospital, a young mother with bone cancer thought she would die when a new tumour attached itself to her spine. There was little the doctors could do. In October 1999 something strange happened: scans showed the growth was shrinking. Then it disappeared completely. The specialist could not explain her recovery. The young mother could – prayer, and the peace that it brought her, made her well again.

Examples on this page adapted from 'Why doctors now believe faith heals', *Reader's Digest.*

The Mantra experiment

In North Carolina, USA, a heart surgeon realised that there was a very low mortality rate among those of his heart patients who came from a very strong Christian community – 3 per cent compared with the expected 33 per cent. Were their faith and the prayers of others making a difference?

An experiment in prayer and healing – under scientific conditions – was set up. It involved: 750 patients with serious heart conditions; 9 hospitals; 20 heart surgeons; and 12 prayer groups of different faiths and in different countries.

Patients were selected at random by the researchers. Immediately they were brought in for surgery, the message went out to the prayer groups worldwide. Groups included: Buddhist monks, nuns in a convent, a Muslim group, various Christian individuals and small groups; also e-mail messages were placed in the Western Wall in Jerusalem (see page 102). The praying began.

Results published, September 2003

- No significant difference overall in the long-term health of those who were prayed for and those who were not.
- Patients who were prayed for tended to be less stressed.
- Some evidence that when the additional prayer groups were set up, this had a beneficial effect on patients' recovery.

The experiment continues.

Certainly in terms of disease, science has been incredible . . . we have increased life expectancy by almost two-thirds in the twentieth century, mostly because of science. But we've put all our eggs in one basket. Science is not the total picture.

Professor of medicine in Washington.

Task 5

Discuss:

1 Using the information on this page, explain what the professor (above) means.
2 Why do you think some doctors are becoming more interested in religion as a means of healing?
3 Do you think faith can heal? Why/why not?
4 Now record the ideas discussed on these two pages as a concept map. You could either start a new mini-concept map or add a new branch to your existing map, entitled 'Spirituality'.

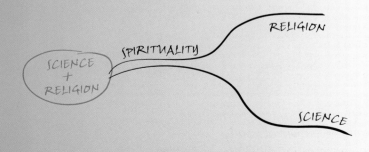

● Can you be a scientist and be religious?

The answer is 'yes'. There are many religious scientists. Two are quoted on this page.

These sources could be summed up in two sentences: Science asks how; religion asks why. The Bible is not a science book; it is more like a poetry book.

Even when religion and science appear to be in head-on contradiction, some people still find a way of believing in both.

I

... I believe that mankind is still evolving and is becoming more sensible and more humane – despite the dramatic backward lurches that occur from time to time. At the religious level, like many other people, I believe in God, despite the absence of positive proof. My own work in the astronomical field, which of course has to do with the enormity of the universe, leads me to feel there must be some purpose in it all.

Sir Arnold Wolfendale FRS, Astronomer Royal 1991–95 and Emeritus Professor of Physics at Durham University.

J

Science asks how things have happened, religion asks why. Genesis is not there to give short, technical answers about how the universe began. It gives us the big answer that things exist because of God's will. One can perfectly well believe in the Big Bang, but believe in it as well as the will of God the creator.

John Polkinghorne, a Christian and a scientist at Cambridge University.

K

At the beginning of the Bible, in the book of Genesis, there are wonderful stories that help us understand why human beings are here at all. I believe, as a result of modern scientific discoveries, that human beings are here because of millions and million years of gradual evolution ...

... And the Bible stories want to tell us that however the world came into existence, whatever scientific process was involved, in the end it all depends, moment by moment for its existence, upon the undergirding and sustaining power of God.

Richard Harris, Bishop of Oxford.

Final task

So . . . has science ditched God?

Through this unit you should have been gradually adding to your 'Science and Religion' concept map. This is a reminder of the kind of thing you are aiming for. This is only half-finished. Yours doesn't need to look like this but you ought to use some of the main branches.

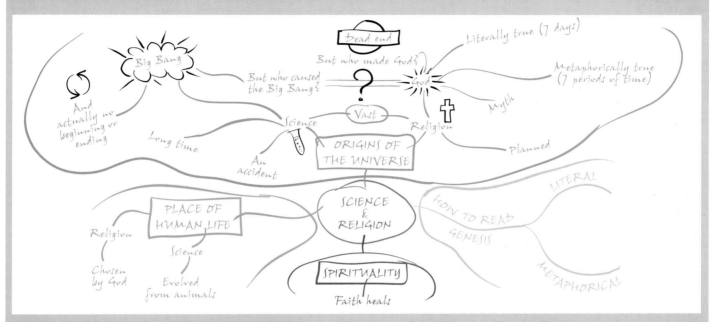

Stage 1 Complete your concept map
Now it is time to apply the finishing touches.
a) If you made mini-concept maps try to combine them together on a single diagram.
b) Add a summary of the ideas on the opposite page.
c) Flip back over the rest of the unit to see if any more ideas jump out at you that you would like to include.
d) Compare your map with a partner's to see if you can learn anything from them.
NB It does not matter at all if your concept map does not look neat – all that matters is that it summarises the main points of the unit as you see them.

Stage 2 Analyse the arguments
Once you are happy that your concept map summarises the main ideas it is time to analyse it. Think about:
a) Your overall view – do you think that there is room for both science and religion or do you think science has ditched religion?

b) What is the strongest argument supporting your view? Find this on your concept map and box it in a bright colour.
c) From that coloured box add connecting lines to any other ideas that support your view.
d) Identify the strongest argument against your view.
e) Box that in a different colour.
f) Identify any area of your concept map that you think is a little vague or unclear – circle that in a third colour.

Stage 3 Write an explanation of your views
You could use the following framework:

I agree/disagree with the view that science has ditched God
My strongest reason is...
One other important reason is...
I understand that others might disagree with me, particularly because....
One thing I am still unsure about and need to investigate further is...

5 Does suffering make it impossible to believe in God?

This is an extract from a play about the civil war in Bosnia. It is based on events that really happened in the early 1990s. Communities were divided and turned on each other. The Serbs wanted to claim land they regarded as theirs. To do so, they started to drive out those of other racial and religious groups. This 'ethnic cleansing' led to the deaths of thousands and forced others to flee as refugees. In this extract, Mirad Balic tells us what happened when Serbian soldiers forced some men into a minefield.

. . . That day, about fifty men and boys were taken for a 'technical expedition' they said.
We walked out of the city and reached a field full of clover.
We had to stand next to each other and join hands.
Then the Serbs told us to walk slowly into the cloverfield.
Suddenly one of the prisoners, Mister Poljac, the father of my friend Ante, cried out, 'Don't do it, don't go, the field is heavily mined.'
As he cried out he was shot.
Nobody was allowed to pick him up, not even Ante.
Then we walked into the mined field.
Never before had I been so afraid, not all my life, because every step could be your last. But I was most afraid for my father, that he would step on a mine.
My father didn't walk beside me, that was forbidden, he was at a distance at the end of the line.
The line was a bit curved so that I could see him.
I was glad about that.
And then it happened.
I looked at the ground for I saw something small sticking out and I was afraid it was a mine.
Then I heard a loud explosion.

Outcomes By the end of this unit you will:

* identify different types of suffering and some of the causes
* identify your own questions about suffering
* evaluate Christian and Buddhist beliefs about suffering
* give your opinion about God and suffering, making reference to religious viewpoints.

Literacy Write a letter as a personal response, discuss in groups, write a fortune line, write statements on cards and sort them, write a personal opinion.

Final task A card-sorting exercise to reflect on suffering and its effects on your own and others' belief in God. A personal response to the statement 'Suffering makes it too hard to believe in God'.

Task 1

1 Read the extract several times. In your own words explain what happened to Mirad.
2 Write a series of questions you'd like to ask Mirad if you were interviewing him in a TV chat show.
3 Start preparing for your final task. Here are two statements that could apply to Mirad's story: **God cannot exist – no God would allow such suffering. Don't blame God for suffering, blame human beings.**

   Discuss them with a partner. Then write down which of the two statements **you** agree with and why.

Somebody had stepped on a mine.

I looked to my father but all I saw was a cloud of mud and blood.
I shouted 'Daddy' and I ran without thinking right over the field to the spot where my father had walked.
Then, one right after another, there were more explosions.
Everybody wanted to run away in panic but the Serbs were still behind us and started to shoot with machine guns.
All over the field were dead bodies and wounded people.
Some men were crying horribly because their arms or legs had been blown off by a mine.
So the Serbs left the engine of their tank running, very loudly, so that nobody could hear the shooting and crying any more.

They kept shooting until nobody walked over the clover field any more.
Then they left.
I was lying very still all the time as if I was shot at the first firing.
But also because I'd found the finger of my father, the hand with the little finger without a nail.
So I knew he was dead.
I felt dead too.
All the shooting and the crying didn't bother me any more.
I don't know how long I lay in the clover field holding my father's hand in my hand.

When it grew dark I stood up.
I buried my father's hand and started walking away from Foca.
    From *Mirad: A Boy From Bosnia* by Ad de Bont.

● What are the causes of suffering?

Suffering is all around us. The photos show some examples: some extreme, some trivial. You can probably think of many others.

A

Potty time at an AIDS orphanage in Kenya.

B

Ouch!

C

Near a feeding station in famine-stricken Somalia.

D

Football fans watch England go out of the World Cup.

E

Flood at Sondrio in Italy.

F

After the genocide in Rwanda.

G

Humorous protest about a serious matter: the impact of passive smoking. This entertainer died from it.

Task 2

1 Discuss Photos **A–G** with a partner then use a table like this to classify them.

Photo	Type(s) of suffering: physical, emotional or psychological	Natural causes or human causes?	Order	Reason
A				
B				
C				
D				
E				
F				
G				

2 All suffering is serious, but some instances are more serious than others.
Rank the examples from 1–7 in order of seriousness (1 is most serious, 7 is least).
You will need to work out some criteria, for example, is suffering more serious if it affects more people, or if it affects children . . .? Fill in columns 4 and 5.

3 Here are two statements that could apply to suffering:

- Humans cause suffering.
- Suffering is an inevitable part of the natural world.

Could they both be true?

● How does suffering affect belief in God?

If God doesn't intervene to stop suffering then:

ALL-POWERFUL?

Maybe God can't actually do anything to stop human suffering.

So

Maybe God is not all-powerful after all.

 OR

Maybe God chooses to be powerless.

God sets natural laws in motion then chooses not to interfere.

God gives humans free will to behave as they wish. Sometime suffering results but you can't have free will without that risk.

ALL-LOVING?

Maybe God does not care about human suffering.

So

Maybe God is not all-loving after all.

 OR

Maybe there is a purpose to all suffering. Good can come out of suffering. We just can't see it yet.

ALL-KNOWING?

Maybe God doesn't even know about human suffering.

So

Maybe God isn't all-knowing after all.

 OR

Maybe God knows so much more than us that God can see the whole picture and the whole of time. God knows what is good in the long run for everyone.

THE PROBLEM   **THE REPLY**

Task 3

In small groups, discuss:

What would a world completely without suffering be like? 'There would be no more....' In your group, list the characteristics of such a world and decide if it would be a good or a bad thing.

● What about natural suffering?

For some believers, suffering caused by humans is not a challenge to their faith in a good and loving God. It can be explained. After all, if God gave humans the freedom to choose, then the blame is theirs not God's.

But hurricanes, floods, earthquakes and famine are often called natural disasters. These pose a particular problem for believers. Why does God allow these? There are two kinds of explanation. The first kind is the right column of the chart on the opposite page.

The second kind is more practical. They ask, 'How natural is this suffering?' Human beings are exploiting and destroying the natural resources of the Earth – deforestation, climate change, pollution and so on. Many rich countries do little to support the poor or to share the world's resources fairly. This could mean that the suffering caused by natural disasters is the result of human beings interfering with nature and that they, not God, are to blame. Are natural disasters just human-made suffering in disguise?

Task 4

Look at headlines **1–8**. Which of these are 'natural' suffering? Give each one a mark out of 10, where 1 is totally natural suffering and 10 is totally human-made suffering. Think hard about this. Most of them are a bit of a mix.

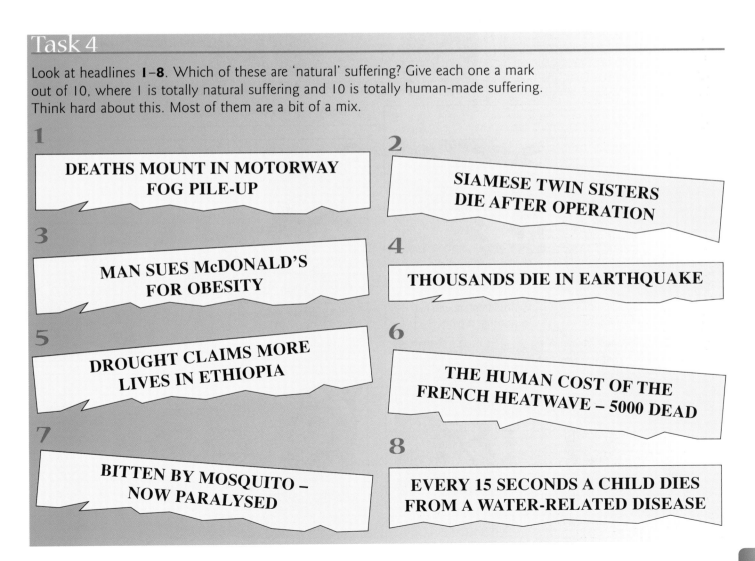

1
DEATHS MOUNT IN MOTORWAY FOG PILE-UP

2
SIAMESE TWIN SISTERS DIE AFTER OPERATION

3
MAN SUES McDONALD'S FOR OBESITY

4
THOUSANDS DIE IN EARTHQUAKE

5
DROUGHT CLAIMS MORE LIVES IN ETHIOPIA

6
THE HUMAN COST OF THE FRENCH HEATWAVE – 5000 DEAD

7
BITTEN BY MOSQUITO – NOW PARALYSED

8
EVERY 15 SECONDS A CHILD DIES FROM A WATER-RELATED DISEASE

● What does the story of Job teach about suffering?

The story of Job is shared by Judaism, Christianity and Islam (Muslims call him Ayyub).

Job is a contented and successful farmer with a large family. His children give parties and have a great life. Job doesn't know he is about to become the subject of a private bet between Satan and God.

So...**suffering is a test of faith.**

3 DISASTER!

a) His animals are killed or captured by enemies.

b) His children are crushed to death at a party.

c) He is penniless and distraught.

d) But Job did not blame God.

6 God has the wisdom. God has the answers.

7 Then God speaks to Job:

This is not because you have sinned.

Why then?

I will ask the questions, you shall answer.

8 Where were you when I laid the Earth's foundations? Tell me, if you know and understand. Who settled its dimensions? Surely you know... Did you proclaim the rules that govern the heavens or determine the laws of nature on Earth?

I know you can do all things and that nothing is impossible for you.

9 God never explains to Job why he suffered. But Job seems satisfied that whatever has happened, it was still in God's control.

10

a) Job's health recovers.

b) His business recovers.

c) He is rich again.

d) He has many children.

So all ends well – apart from the pain Job must have felt at the loss of his first family and his own terrible experiences. But this is a story well over 2000 years old. It is a story which shows that human beings have long struggled with the question, 'Why does God allow suffering, particularly for good people?' Job concluded that **suffering is not a punishment. God is in control, God has a plan – even though there are many things human beings do not, and cannot, understand.**

Task 5

Do a 'fortune line' for Job – your teacher may give you a sheet to help you.

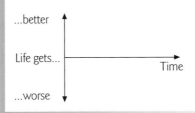

● Rosalind Grimshaw: overcoming suffering

Artist Rosalind Grimshaw discovered she had Parkinson's disease in her mid-thirties. Her doctors told her she would be fine for about ten years and then her health would deteriorate badly.

By the mid-1990s, Rosalind was spending most of the day immobile or unable to control her body's jerking. She says, 'I was at a very, very low ebb, desolate and despondent most of the time. But I clung to the belief that I would be able to do my work properly again one day . . . and I created designs in my head. I knew I mustn't give up.'

Then, new drugs were tried and gradually Rosalind found it possible to work again for part of the day, starting in the early hours. She entered and won a competition to design and create the Creation Window for Chester Cathedral (see the finished window opposite).

Rosalind designed the smaller panels of the window when in hospital. She used coloured paper for the stained glass. The medical staff displayed the panels in the ward for people to enjoy!

Rosalind working with stained glass.

1 It was a fantastically creative period for me. It has also been a chance to recognise how, in spite of all the distress and frustration the disease gives me, there are ways in which it has actually helped me with this work. It has made me slow down and focus completely in a way I might not have done with more mobility.

2 Some days I was able to draw on the glass and cut loads, but others I would be wiggling all over the place or else I couldn't move. . . . But . . . anxiety makes the Parkinson's symptoms worse, so you have to be very tough with yourself.

3 In my own life, I feel that making this window has brought about amazing changes in me that amount to a kind of healing.

4 The sun coming up every morning is like a daily promise of hope, even if it is hidden behind clouds and rain.

The information and quotations on these pages come from *Six Days: The story of the making of the Chester Cathedral Creation Window*, published by Alastair Sawday.

Task 6

1 Read quotations **1–4** above. In which ways has Rosalind's suffering had positive outcomes – for herself and others? List at least three ideas.

2 Do some research to find out about another person who achieved something positive, despite suffering in some way. Write three slides about that person for a PowerPoint presentation.

Slide a) What was the suffering?

Slide b) What was achieved despite it?

Slide c) What did their story teach you about suffering?

For each of the six days of the Genesis creation story, there is a main window. Beneath each one, there is a smaller panel linking it to the modern world. Creation is ongoing. As human beings create things, they need to take their responsibility for the planet seriously.

Hovering above the centre is the white dove representing the spirit of God.

The hand of God spreads across the first five days of creation.

Then, on the sixth day, humans are created and take control. The human hand reaches out to God in the last panel.

As the light changes during the day, so the hand of God reflects all over the cathedral walls.

Beneath the creation of light on Day 1, the small window shows modern technology lighting the darkness – lights from traffic coming and going as well as skyscrapers lit up.

Beneath the creation of human life on Day 6 are: a foetus in the womb; DNA spirals; and twin serpents symbolising medicine and the knowledge of good and evil.

● **What does Buddhism teach about suffering?**

A response that doesn't involve God

Suffering troubles some believers in God. But what if God doesn't exist? Would this make suffering easier to understand?

Questions about suffering gave rise to Buddhism two and a half thousand years ago in Northern India. You may already know the story of Prince Siddattha Gotama.

Protected from reality, with a lavish lifestyle and a happy marriage, he still felt a sense of dissatisfaction about life. Seeing three ageing, diseased and dead men left him with questions about suffering and its causes. He wondered, 'How can people be truly contented when the realities of life are so awful?' And for himself, he wondered, 'If a life of luxury cannot bring contentment, what can?'

Having seen a holy man on his search for meaning, Siddattha left the palace to seek answers to those questions. After six years of wandering, his enlightenment came through a long night of meditation. Finally, he understood the truth about suffering and started to teach The Four Noble Truths. After this experience, he became known as the Buddha, the enlightened one. Buddhism was born.

Task 7

The Four Noble Truths – what do you think?

The chart below sets out the Buddha's teaching about suffering and how to live. Read each 'Truth' and then answer the questions in 'Your thoughts?'.

The Noble Truth	Your thoughts?
1 Suffering cannot be avoided. (It means more than pain; it includes a sense of life not being perfect.)	Make a quick list of different kinds of suffering – look back at page 63 to remind you. Do you know anybody who has had a life free from **any** kind of suffering? What is the worst kind?
2 Suffering is caused by greed, hatred and ignorance. (Basically, by being selfish.)	List the sort of suffering that comes out of greed, hatred and ignorance. Does your list cover all sorts of suffering? If not, what questions would you ask a Buddhist about the causes of suffering?
3 Suffering will cease to trouble you when you accept that it is part of life and when you lose your selfish desires.	Using your same list from **2**, discuss with a partner what would happen if the greed had been turned into giving, the hatred into kindness and the ignorance into understanding. Why are we selfish? Can we really change?
4 There is a path to follow that will help you lose these selfish desires. It is called the Eightfold Path and sets out practical ways of living.	What sort of help do you think you and others need to help you live in a less self-centred way? The guidance given in the Eightfold Path includes developing the right attitude of mind and heart, through meditation and showing compassion for others. Find out more about this Path and then work out your own eight pathways to reduce suffering.

How does this work in real life?

Joyce Miller is a Buddhist. These are some of the things she believes about suffering:

I don't see suffering as an issue . . . it's just a fact. It just is. Life is very hard, and suffering, or the unsatisfactoriness of life, needs to be dealt with, but because Buddhism isn't based on belief in God, suffering isn't a theological [about God] issue. For the same reason, Buddhism feels no need to explain the presence of suffering in the world. It is simply a fact which has to be faced and Buddhism is about... how you deal with suffering as it arises . . .

I once talked to a Buddhist who had cancer and she said, 'I just came to the conclusion that I had it. No point in thinking "Why me?"' As soon as she accepted that she had it, all sorts of other things were much easier to cope with. But she also talked about how hard it was . . . Your illness is going to be managed by your mind, so it's your mind you have to work on.

You do this by stilling the mind in meditation and following the EIGHTFOLD PATH which shows the way to end suffering.

Task 8

Job and the Buddha found different ways of dealing with suffering. Job's way involved God; the Buddha's didn't.

Discuss the following two statements in a small group:

- Suffering? Only God knows everything. (Job)
- Suffering? Only human beings can find the solution. (the Buddha)

There are never easy answers to suffering, but which of the two views do you support most? Why?

● **What does Christianity teach about suffering?**

This story sums up one very important belief of Christians – a belief which helps some of them cope with the issue of suffering. Although most religions teach that there is one God, only Christians make the claim about God and suffering that is in this story. What is the claim?
Read the story . . .

The Long Silence

At the end of time, billions of people were scattered on a great plain before God's throne. Most shrank from the brilliant light before them; some groups near the front talked heatedly, not with cringing shame, but with belligerence.

'Can God judge us? How can He know about suffering?' snapped a young woman. She ripped open a sleeve to reveal a tattooed number from a concentration camp. 'We endured terror, beating, and death.'

In another group, a young black boy lowered his collar. 'What about this?' he demanded, showing an ugly rope burn. 'Lynched for no crime but being black.'

In another crowd a pregnant schoolgirl with sullen eyes. 'Why should I suffer?' she murmured. 'It wasn't my fault.'

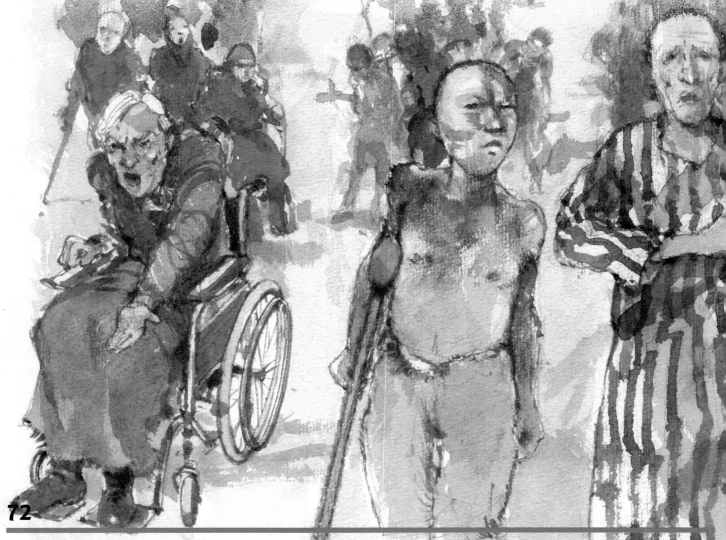

Far out across the plain were hundreds of similar groups; each had a complaint against God for the evil and suffering permitted in his world. How lucky God was to live in heaven where all was sweetness and light, where there was no weeping or fear, no hunger or hatred. What did God know of all that people had been forced to endure in the world? For God lives a pretty sheltered life, they said.

So each picked the person from their group who had suffered the most and sent them to confront God: a Jew, a black person, a person from Hiroshima, a child from Chernobyl, a severely disabled person, a person with Aids, a rape victim. In the centre of the plain they consulted with each other. At last they were ready to present their case. It was rather clever.

Before God could be qualified to be their judge, He must endure what they had endured. Their decision was that God should be sentenced to live on earth as a man.

Let him be a Jew. Give him work so difficult that his family think he is out of his mind when he tries to do it. Let him live in a war-torn occupied country. Let him be betrayed by his closest friends. Let him face false charges, be tried by a prejudiced jury and convicted by a cowardly judge. Let him be tortured. At last let him see what it means to be terribly alone. Then let him die a slow, humiliating death with many witnesses watching him suffer.

As each leader made their contribution there were loud murmurs of approval from the assembled gathering. When the last had finished pronouncing their sentence there was a long silence. No one moved.

For suddenly they all knew . . .

Task 9

Remember this is a story that takes place at the end of time.

1 The final sentence of this story has been left unfinished. Complete it in a way that makes the meaning of this story clear.
2 Write the meaning in a statement that can be added to the set of statements in the final task (page 74).
3 Why do you think the story helps Christians when they think about suffering?

Final task

Preparation

1 Read through all the statements opposite. You have seen all the ideas before! If in doubt, look back through the unit or check out the pictures on this page.

2 The statements should be written out on paper/card. Your teacher may provide these. In small groups, sort them into two sets:
- statements which make it hard to believe in God (for example, God is powerless)
- statements which do not make it hard to believe in God (for example, Humans cause suffering).

You may have some that you're not sure about – leave those out.

3 Working on your own, choose your five most convincing statements from each set.

4 Finally, decide which set of five you will use to answer the following question:

So . . . does suffering make it impossible to believe in God?

Write your personal answer to that question, using this framework.

- My **opinion** is that . . . *(one sentence to make it clear)*
- I agree with the following **statements**. *(list them)*
- The **reasons** I have chosen them are . . . *(explain why)*
- I think these **examples** from real life help support my opinion. *(give examples from the unit, from the news or from your own personal experience)*
- I can understand some statements giving **different points of view** . . . *(list the other five you chose)*
- The most convincing case they made was . . .
- I found the **ideas/beliefs** in the **Jewish, Buddhist** and **Christian responses** to suffering helpful/unhelpful because . . . *(refer to at least one idea from each religion)*

The case studies on pages 68–69 and 76–77 can give you some extra ideas. One shows how suffering is overcome by an individual; the other is an example of how groups/organisations work to relieve the suffering of others.

God cannot exist – no God would allow such suffering.

Don't blame God for suffering, blame human beings.

Humans cause suffering.

Suffering is an inevitable part of the natural world.

God is all-powerful but doesn't intervene to stop suffering.

God is powerless.

God knows what is good for everyone in the long run.

God is not good.

God knows everything about suffering.

God doesn't stop it so God doesn't care.

God understands human suffering because Jesus was God and he suffered more than most humans ever suffer.

It would be a better world if no one suffered in the first place.

There is no explanation good enough for the suffering of the innocent.

Suffering caused by natural disasters proves there is no God.

God set natural laws in motion and does not interfere.

The suffering caused by natural disasters is the result of human beings interfering with nature. They, not God, are to blame.

Suffering is God's punishment for sin.

Suffering is not a punishment from God.

God cares enough to have given us free will. Suffering may result.

Suffering is meant as a test of faith.

God is in control, God has a plan, even though there are many things human beings do not, and cannot, understand.

Suffering is caused by greed, hatred and ignorance.

Good can come out of suffering.

Suffering will cease to trouble you when you accept that it is part of life and when you lose your selfish desires.

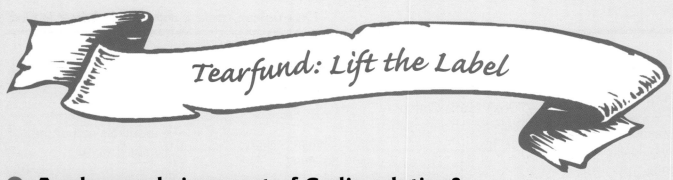

Tearfund: Lift the Label

● Are human beings part of God's solution?

There is massive suffering in the world: the suffering of poverty, brought about by unjust governments, by the consequences of natural disasters and by the failure of human beings to bring about fair systems of trade. It is no secret. These images are constantly in the media.

All religions teach a duty to care about others. The golden rule – 'Love your neighbour as you love yourself' – is a shared value.

Tearfund is a Christian group that believes in action on behalf of the world's poor. Why? Tearfund would say the Bible is full of evidence that God demands justice for the poor. For example, 'Speak up for those who cannot speak for themselves, for the rights of all who are destitute. Speak up and judge fairly; defend the rights of the poor and needy.' (Proverbs 31.8–9.) Read about one of Tearfund's campaigns.

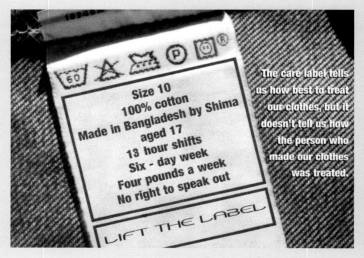

The care label tells us how best to treat our clothes, but it doesn't tell us how the person who made our clothes was treated.

Tearfund's 'Lift the label' campaign involves all ages but there is a special focus on young people because of their consumer power.

Ours are not the first hands to touch our clothes. Before we touch them they have been produced and handled by many others, people with names, faces, children and parents who, like us, are made in the image of God. But unlike us, they are paid low wages, work long hours and in appalling conditions . . . We plan fashion events to enable young people here in the UK to see the people behind the clothes they buy and to use their consumer power to bring about positive change.

Anne Kirke, Tearfund's Youth Events Co-ordinator.

The people who produce the jeans which end up in our shops are often living in the world's poorest countries and are often the most disadvantaged people in those countries.

Shima

Shima is 17 years old. She has worked in a clothes factory in Dhaka, Bangladesh for three years. Her job is to put buttonholes on jeans and jackets. Many of the clothes she makes end up in UK stores. Shima works from 8 a.m. to 8 or 9 p.m., 6 days a week. She earns 425 Taka a week, just £4.40. She would need twice that amount to live on to be able to afford basic essentials like food, healthcare and accommodation.

Shima at work.

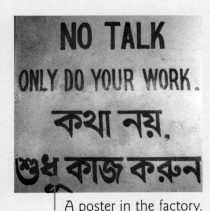
A poster in the factory.

The information and images on this spread are from Tearfund.

Task

1 Discuss in a small group:
  How far should you feel guilty or responsible when buying a pair of jeans?
2 In groups, research an organisation, or an individual, working to relieve the suffering of the poor. Present your research in the form of a word-processed booklet with a summary of key points. The key points are:

• The aims/beliefs of the organisation/individual
• Some of the ways they have helped.

Here are some websites that might help you. Some are religious groups, others non-religious.

www.tearfund.org	www.cafod.org.uk	www.oxfam.org.uk
www.christian-aid.org.uk	www.muslimaid.org	www.redcross.org.uk
www.khalsaaid.org	www.islamic-relief.com	www.tzedek.org.uk
www.dfid.gov.uk	www.wateraid.org.uk	

6 Good versus evil!

● Good versus evil in daily life

1 Craig notices someone drop a ten pound note in the street. He picks it up, but does not run after the person who dropped it. Instead he gives it to a homeless person who is begging nearby.

2 There is a national appeal for funds to help the starving in Ethiopia. **Anna** turns the TV pictures off – she's seen it all before. Instead, she goes into town to buy the latest designer trainers.

3 Amy gets up early to get her mum a cup of tea.

4 Steve observes how a pupil in his class is regularly getting bullied out of sight of staff. The pupil is now missing school. Steve does nothing.

5 Holly challenges a racist joke.

6 Sarah's boyfriend has some ecstasy tablets. Her friend, **Becky**, persuades her not to take one.

7 Ronan takes part in a sponsored fun run for Red Nose Day and raises a lot of money, but he keeps some for himself.

8 Ben meets up with Year 6 kids and lets them smoke his cigarettes – 20p a puff.

Outcomes By the end of this unit you will:
- explain what is meant by good and evil
- express your own thoughts and feelings on good and evil in the world and in your own life
- know some Christian, Hindu and humanist religious points of view about the cause of evil
- decide if you think the existence of evil is a barrier to believing in God.

Literacy Write a personal response, discuss in groups, comment on a modern tale, research using websites, write notes to accompany an image.

Final task Express the conflict between good and evil in a PowerPoint presentation.

Summary task for Units 3–6 Debate on reasons to believe or not to believe in God.

Task 1A

1 In groups, use the criteria in the 'You need to know' box to sort the situations
(**1**–**8**) into three groups:

Good	Evil	Not sure

2 For each of the 'Good' and 'Evil' sets, try to find three things they have in
common. For the 'Not sure' set, see if any of them mix the criteria and explain
why you cannot make up your mind.

3 Choose one situation that interests you. Go back a step to the point before the
action takes place – there is a choice to be made between a good option and a bad
one. Follow both options through to possible outcomes, as in a game of
Consequences. For example:

Hear racist joke	**Hear racist joke**
Good option	Bad option
_____	_____
_____	_____
Outcome	Outcome
_____	_____
_____	_____

4 Discuss: Is saying or doing nothing about evil in itself evil?

Task 1B

Maybe you think evil is too strong a word for actions like these.
Maybe there is a difference between something that is simply wrong
and something that is evil. Over the next twelve pages you will explore
in detail what people mean by good and evil.

At the end of the unit, your final task will be to prepare a
PowerPoint presentation showing your understanding of these
issues and your beliefs.

To help you with your final task you will be prompted on each
spread to draft one slide summarising it. You may have your own ideas
but it should at least include one picture and three bullet points like this.
To start, draft a slide entitled: 'Good versus evil in daily life'.

Good versus evil in daily life

- *Examples of
  everyday good*
- *Examples of
  everyday evil*
- *Examples which
  combine*

● Good versus evil in fantasy

The battle between good and evil is big news in fiction, art, film and TV.
Bookshops find that stories about witches, magic, good and evil are very
popular. The struggle between the good and the bad has always been
there in all the popular children's stories – and adult stories too.

The Wicked Witch of the West from *The Wizard of Oz*

Dorothy is the innocent traveller in the Land
of Oz, trying to help the friends that she meets
there. The Wicked Witch of the West aims to
thwart her plans by keeping her prisoner.
Dorothy eventually kills the witch by throwing
water over her. One of the other witches is, by
contrast, very good and helps Dorothy to return
home by giving her the magic red shoes.

Sauron from the film series of *Lord of the Rings*

Sauron is the Dark Lord. When the One Ring
was cut from his hand at a great Battle he lost
his body. Now he is formless but terrifying – just
a great Eye, surrounded by flame. His gaze means
instant death. He lives in his tower of Barad-dûr
where he is gathering strength to begin the long
search for the Ring – the only thing that can
restore him and return his power. Without a
body he is no more than a terrible will. Good
is represented by the fellowship of the Ring.

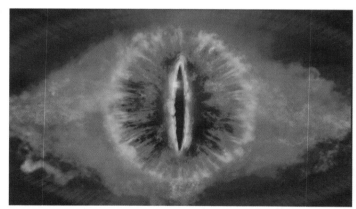

Task 2A

Work in pairs.

1 For the examples given here (or
using your own favourite example)
fill out a table like this one. If there
are many different characters who
might be good or evil choose the
lead character.

2 Discuss: What impression does
this give you of the battle between
good and evil? Is it scary or is it
entertaining or funny?

	Good	Evil
Name		
Background - anything that is relevant		
Characteristics – personality or physical features		
Special Powers		
Motivation – what are they hoping to achieve?		
Results – do they win in the end or lose or draw? And what are the consequences for others? If you don't know, say what you expect to happen and why.		

The White Witch from *The Lion, the Witch and the Wardrobe*

The White Witch puts a spell on Narnia to make it always winter. Aslan the lion is her great enemy. He comes to free Narnia from the spell but the White Witch kills him. However he rises from the dead and leads the good Narnians in battle against the White Witch and her evil followers.

Spike from *Buffy the Vampire Slayer*

Buffy is a vampire slayer. She aims to protect people by killing vampires. Spike is a vampire. He is called Spike because he put the heads of his victims on spikes. He has tried to kill Buffy many times. However a secret government group called The Initiative kidnap Spike and put a chip in his brain which makes him unable to kill innocent people. So Spike becomes good – by force – and he falls in love with Buffy, who wants nothing to do with him.

Task 2B

Your final task will be to prepare a PowerPoint presentation showing your understanding of good and evil.

Draft a second slide entitled: 'Good versus evil in fantasy'.

> **Good versus evil in fantasy**
>
> *Choose one example only and summarise*
> - *Representing good*
> - *Representing evil*
> - *Impression of the struggle*

● Good versus evil in the real world

You have only to watch the TV news or pick up a history book to know that there is and always has been evil in the real world. Sometimes it is extreme as in the case of the slaughter of the Jews in the Holocaust during the Second World War. Sometimes it is more subtle or hidden as in child abuse within the family but still with very damaging effects.

You are less likely to find 'good news' in the newspapers or on TV. You sometimes have to supply the good news stories yourself.

Sources **A–G** show good and evil in the modern world. You will be able to think of many examples yourself. There are others on page 78.

Task 3A

Work in pairs. Choose three sources from this spread. Discuss the flash question that is with each one, then write your answer to these questions:
1 What is evil in this story (if there is any)?
2 Who is to blame for the evil? The person who did it or the society (parents, community, school) that created that person?
3 What is the good in this story (if there is any)?
4 Who is responsible for the good? The person who did it or the society (parents, community, school) that created that person?
5 Do you feel you have any power yourself to affect any of the situations shown on this spread?

A

> How has she depicted evil?

This picture is painted by a child who suffered abuse in a violent home.

B

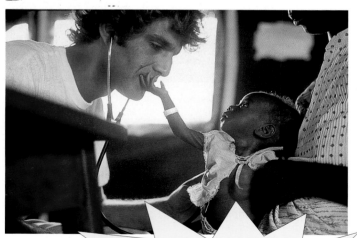

> Does the increasing need for aid workers show that there is more evil in the world than there was or more good?

These two people have given their working lives to helping people in poor countries live healthier lives. These are just two of the hundreds of thousands of aid workers around the world. It is estimated that there are more people working in humanitarian aid now than at virtually any time in human history.

C

CHILDREN SOLD INTO SLAVERY

Who is evil? The parents who sold these children? The traders who bought them and make them work? The clients who buy the products they make?

D

What difference will this project make to the children? What difference might it make to the city?

These street children in Brazil are creating a garden and growing food in the middle of Curitiba.

E

TERRORIST USED INTERNET TO GET BOMB-MAKING INFORMATION

Does this make the internet evil?

G

'DOZENS WATCHED WHILE FOUR RACIST THUGS BEAT ME UP IN BROAD DAYLIGHT'

Is standing by and doing nothing evil?

F

The hurt boy and the birds

The hurt boy talked to the birds
and fed them the crumbs of his heart.

It was not easy to find the words
for secrets he hid under his skin.
The hurt boy spoke of a bully's fist
that made his face a bruised moon —
his spectacles stamped to ruin.

It was not easy to find the words
for things that nightly hissed
as if his pillow was a hideaway for creepy-crawlies
— the note sent to the girl he fancied
held high in mockery.

But the hurt boy talked to the birds
and their feathers gave him welcome —

Their wings taught him new ways to become.

John Agard.

What hope has this hurt boy been given?

Task 3B

Draft a third slide for your presentation called 'Good versus evil in the real world'.

Good versus evil in the real world

- *Responsible for evil*
- *Responsible for good*
- *My place in the struggle*

● **Good and evil as forces**

One common religious view is that evil is a force, unseen and out of a control, but very real and affecting every human being. This is a common view in Eastern religions particularly Hinduism.

In Hinduism, there is constant battle between good and evil. To Hindus evil is a force not a person. The battle against evil is symbolised in the murti (image) of Kali. She is shown as the destroyer of evil and punisher of evil-doers (see picture A). But she is only a symbol. She is not the one who beats the power of evil.

Human responsibility

The image of Kali reassures Hindus that good can defeat evil. But it is up to individuals to help this happen. Every small action against evil is part of the struggle. Kali doesn't make this happen. Kali just motivates Hindus to continue in their struggle.

Evil actions have consequences

Hindus believe that:

- what you do today is a direct result of your behaviour in a former life (the law of cause and effect, known as karma);
- your soul (atman) is indestructible but your body can exist in different lives (reincarnation);
- your karma determines how many lives you live;
- your soul 'wanders' from body to body through birth, life, death and re-birth (this cycle is known as samsara);
- you must do good and defeat evil in order to escape samsara and be united with Brahman (this release is known as moksha);
- a good life is achieved by upholding and following the right conduct and laws which make for a good society (this way of life is called dharma).

Kali is often shown as dark and menacing, with her tongue hanging out and with a necklace of skulls and a severed head in her hand. Her four arms represent power. But, like many murtis, she also has one hand held up as a blessing and a reassurance that goodness will replace evil.

Task 4A

1 Read the information carefully and match these words to the correct definition below: samsara; moksha; atman; karma; dharma.

what you are today is the result of what you did in a former life	the cycle of birth, life, death and rebirth	escaping the cycle of samsara
a good way of life		the soul

2 **a)** What are the attractions to you of this explanation of evil?
 b) What are the problems with it?

The bigger picture

In the life of the individual, evil can gradually be defeated, but the cosmic struggle between good and evil will go on forever.

Ladders lead the player up from a virtue closer to moksha, often to a specific 'heaven'. Notice how most of the ladders are near the top of the board and that there are fewer ladders than there are snakes. This makes the game quite hard to get into at first but the chances of finishing improve as players get further up the board.

Snakes lead the player down from a sin to rebirth as an animal. The sins are linked to specific creatures and the worse the sin, the longer the fall. Notice how most of the snakes are in the bottom half of the board, making it difficult to advance to start with and the longest falls come from the few snakes nearest to the finish.

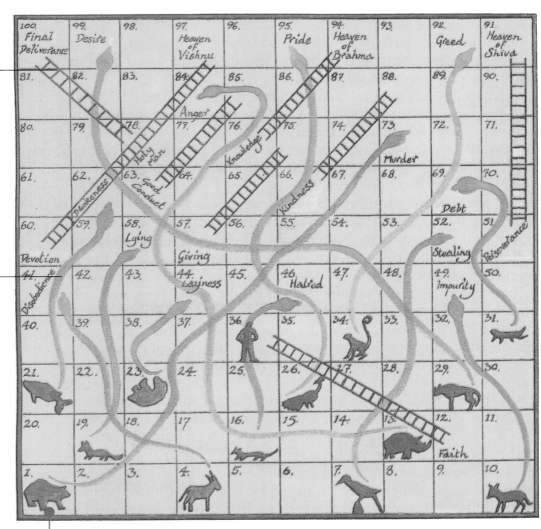

This Hindu game, Moksha Chitram, may look familiar! It shows how your good and evil karma can move you towards or away from moksha.

Task 4B

Choose one picture and write three bullet points for a slide explaining the religious ideas that good and evil are forces.

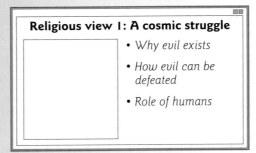

Religious view 1: A cosmic struggle

- *Why evil exists*
- *How evil can be defeated*
- *Role of humans*

● Evil as a 'being'

A different religious view is that evil is a being of some sort. This is Satan or the devil. Images of Satan are common in art: he is shown as a horned beast with a pitchfork and tail. On the right is a picture from a children's magazine called the *Catholic Treasure Box*.

This has been particularly associated with religions such as Christianity and Islam although individual Christians and Muslims will have very different views.

According to traditions Satan is a fallen angel. He was originally part of God's perfect creation. He was the most important angel but he wanted to become ruler of the Earth. So he rebelled against God. He persuaded human beings to disobey God too. He tempted Eve to eat the apple which she had been told not to eat. Sin and evil entered the world because of him (see opposite).

Other angels also followed Satan's lead. Satan became the ruler of this band of fallen angels. They actively promote sinfulness and evil. They tempt ordinary people to disobey God. They bring terror, sickness and suffering wherever they can out of sheer hatred for God and the good world God created.

In the gospels Satan tempts Jesus to disobey God. Jesus was only able to start his teaching and miracles when he has passed this test and resisted Satan. The gospels say Satan blinds those who can't see the good news of Jesus. One of Jesus' most common miracles was to heal people who were possessed by demons under the control of Satan.

After his resurrection Jesus warned his disciples that Satan was going to cause more trouble. Following Jesus' teaching, Paul and Peter – the first leaders of Christianity – warned Christians to be on their guard.

The end of the Christian Bible describes a final battle between God and Satan; this has not yet taken place – it will be at the end of time. Satan himself will be captured and cast into the lake of fire with all the wicked people. They will be punished for their rebellion. The lake of fire will also test, prove and refine those in it. So the story could have a happy ending.

God did not create Satan to fulfil this role. Evil was not part of God's plan. The question remains as to why God allows Satan to continue but . . . God does.

Some people believe this today. They live their lives actively trying to resist Satan's influence. They believe that anything to do with the spirit world – séances, witches, Halloween, even Harry Potter books – is dangerous flirtation with the spirit world which is under the control of Satan. One problem for believers is how do you know when it is Satan tempting you. You can only do this by developing your inner sense of right and wrong or seeking the advice and guidance of others.

Evil might even be a good thing as people can develop their own goodness much better if they are faced with the constant struggle against evil. It keeps them on their toes. It stops them getting complacent.

Your enemy the devil prowls around like a roaring lion looking for someone to devour.

I Peter 5.8.

Finally, my brethren, be strong in the Lord ... Put on the whole armour of God, that you may be able to stand against the devil. For we do not wrestle against flesh and blood, but against the rulers of the darkness of this age.

Ephesians 6.

The story of the Fall

The snake was the most clever of all the wild animals the Lord God had made. One day, the snake spoke to the woman. He said, 'Did God really say that you must not eat fruit from any tree in the garden?'

The woman answered the snake, 'We may eat from the trees in the garden. But God told us, "You must not eat from the tree that is in the middle of the garden. You must not even touch it, or you will die."'

But the snake said to the woman, 'You will not die. God knows that if you eat the fruit from that tree, you will learn about good and evil. Then you will be like God.'

The woman saw that the tree was beautiful. She saw that its fruit was good to eat and that it would make her wise. So she took some of its fruit and ate it. She also gave some of the fruit to her husband, and he ate it.

Then, it was as if the man's and woman's eyes were opened. They realised they were naked, so they sewed fig leaves together and made something to cover themselves.

Then they heard the Lord God walking in the garden . . . And the man and his wife hid from the Lord God.

From Genesis 2 and 3.

Task 5A

I Read the story carefully and match the symbols to these meanings in the story:

- knowledge of good and evil;
- Satan;
- a place of beauty and perfection unmarked by evil.

Task 5B

2 a) What are the attractions to you of this explanation of evil?

   b) What are the problems with it?

3 What are the similarities and differences with the view on pages 84–85?

4 Choose one picture and write three bullet points for a slide summarising the religious ideas that evil is a being.

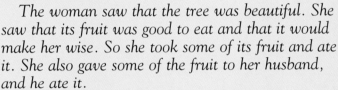

Religious view 2: Satan

- *Why evil exists*
- *How evil can be defeated*
- *Role of humans*

● Evil as a human phenomenon

A third explanation of evil is that it is a creation of human beings. It comes from within, as a result of our choices. This is particularly associated with the Humanists although some religious people also agree with this view for other reasons. Humanists believe the existence of evil is a further reason not to believe in God. A loving god, if one existed, could have made a world where humans had limited free will (just as we have limited physical and mental capacities).

A Humanist perspective on good and evil

As humans we are on our own without God. So:

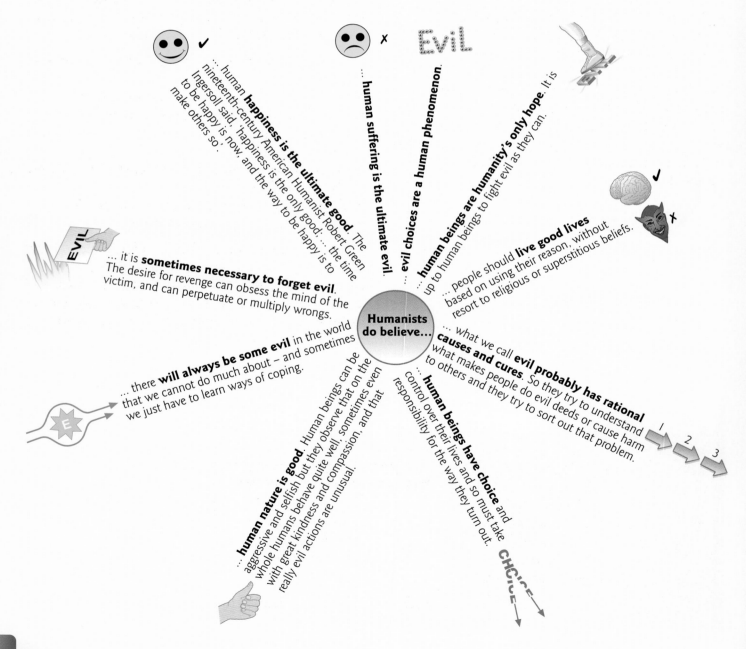

... human **happiness is the ultimate good**. The nineteenth-century American Humanist Robert Green Ingersoll said, 'happiness is the only good: ... the time to be happy is now, and the way to be happy is to make others so'.

... human suffering is the ultimate evil.

... evil choices are a human phenomenon.

... **human beings are humanity's only hope**. It is up to human beings to fight evil as they can.

... people should **live good lives** based on using their reason, without resort to religious or superstitious beliefs.

... it is **sometimes necessary to forget evil**. The desire for revenge can obsess the mind of the victim, and can perpetuate or multiply wrongs.

... what we call **evil probably has rational causes and cures**. So they try to understand what makes people do evil deeds or cause harm to others and they try to sort out that problem.

Humanists do believe...

... there **will always be some evil** in the world that we cannot do much about – and sometimes we just have to learn ways of coping.

... **human beings have choice** and control over their lives and so must take responsibility for the way they turn out.

... **human nature is good**. Human beings can be aggressive and selfish but they observe that on the whole humans behave quite well, sometimes even with great kindness and compassion, and that really evil actions are unusual.

Humanists don't believe...

- in God, or in the supernatural. So no Humanist can accept the idea of evil as a supernatural force, or as something caused by demons or devils.
- that people can be 'born evil' or that evil is inevitable.
- that evil is God's punishment or a test, because they don't think there is a god to punish or test people.
- in an afterlife where evil will be punished and goodness rewarded.
- in evil as part of a divine plan which people have to accept rather than fight.
- some god will help us to end evil.

So...**the way to resist evil is to promote happiness.** To live, vote, choose jobs, relate to other people, spend and invest our money, in ways that respect other people's rights, minimise suffering, and increase yours and their happiness.

Good and evil without religion

Humanists believe that a sense of what is good and evil does not depend on religion. Religion might motivate people to do good and resist evil. But it does not depend on religion. Instead Humanists believe that these values evolve from human experience. If human civilisation were to develop all over again, it is unlikely that exactly the same religions would develop. But it is very likely that our basic moral principles would be the same, because human beings, who have evolved to live in groups, need the kinds of rule which enable us to live together co-operatively and harmoniously. These include:

- looking after the young and other vulnerable people
- valuing the truth and respecting promises
- fair allocation of power and property according to some recognised system which includes merit
- helping each other when threatened or when there are disasters
- disapproving of and punishing wrongdoers
- restraining violence and killing.

All well summed up in the 'Golden Rule': 'Treat other people in a way you would like to be treated yourself'. This is true to human nature and experience. It does not need to be given to us by a deity. It is simple and clear and works well in practice.

Task 6

1 a) What are the attractions to you of this explanation of evil?
  b) What are the problems with it?
2 In what ways is it similar or different to the other two explanations?
3 Find or draw a picture and write three bullet points for a slide explaining the Humanist idea that good and evil are human creations.

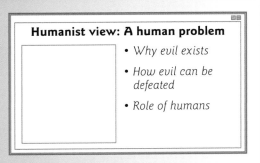

Humanist view: A human problem

- *Why evil exists*
- *How evil can be defeated*
- *Role of humans*

Preparing for your final task

A woman dreamed that she walked into a brand-new shop in the arcade and, to her surprise, found God behind the counter.

'What do you sell here?' she asked.

'Everything your heart desires,' said God.

Hardly daring to believe what she was hearing, the woman decided to ask for the best things a human being could wish for.

'I want peace and love and happiness and freedom from fear,' she said.

Then, as an after-thought, she added, 'Not just for me. For everyone on Earth.'

God smiled. 'I think you've got me wrong, my dear,' he said. 'We don't sell fruits, only seeds.'

Anthony de Mello, *Taking Flight*.

Task 7

1 In this story what do you think are the seeds and the fruits?
2 What would someone who believed that good and evil were forces say were the seed and the fruits? (See page 84.)
3 What would someone who believed that evil was a being say were the seed and the fruits? (See page 86.)
4 What would someone who believed that good and evil were a human phenomenon say were the seed and the fruits? (See page 88.)
5 What might a humanist change in this story?

Final task

You should now have drafted out a number of PowerPoint slides. You can now redraft and add the finishing touches.

Stage 1
1 Think about your own opinion. Which of these explanations do you favour? (Evil as a force, a being or a human phenomenon.)
   And why?
2 Draft a final slide with a picture and an explanation of your opinion.

Stage 2
3 Design a title slide.
4 Choose some background music or sound effects for the presentation: it could be different for each slide.
5 Write notes for your commentary.

Stage 3
Present!

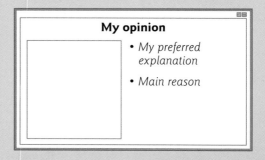

My opinion

- *My preferred explanation*
- *Main reason*

● **Preparing for your debate**

Units 3–6 have worked together. They have given you various ideas that you can use in your debate about the existence of God.

Here is a summary of some important ideas and the counter arguments. Which could you use? You will be able to add your own ideas.

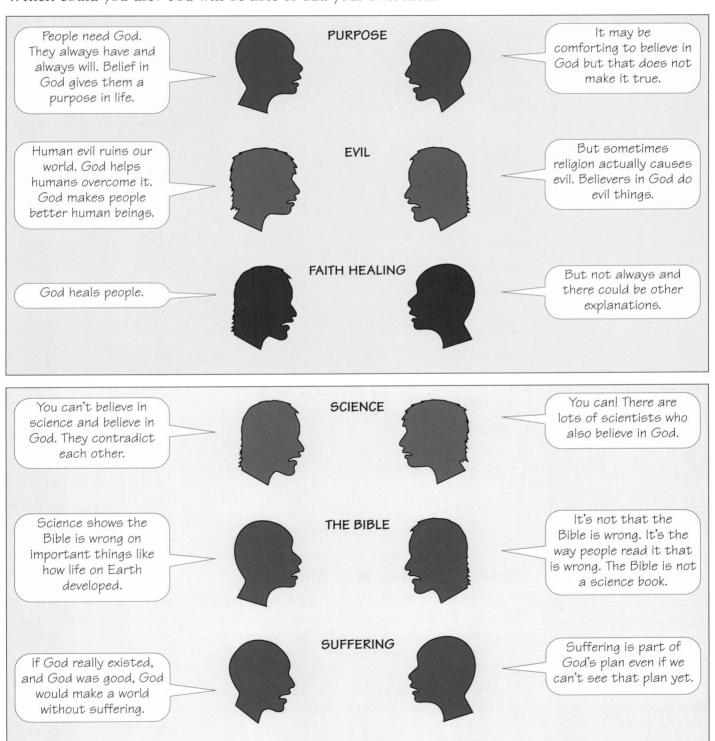

PURPOSE

People need God. They always have and always will. Belief in God gives them a purpose in life.

It may be comforting to believe in God but that does not make it true.

EVIL

Human evil ruins our world. God helps humans overcome it. God makes people better human beings.

But sometimes religion actually causes evil. Believers in God do evil things.

FAITH HEALING

God heals people.

But not always and there could be other explanations.

SCIENCE

You can't believe in science and believe in God. They contradict each other.

You can! There are lots of scientists who also believe in God.

THE BIBLE

Science shows the Bible is wrong on important things like how life on Earth developed.

It's not that the Bible is wrong. It's the way people read it that is wrong. The Bible is not a science book.

SUFFERING

If God really existed, and God was good, God would make a world without suffering.

Suffering is part of God's plan even if we can't see that plan yet.

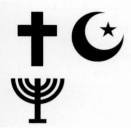

London
22 June

Dear Mr Michael

I am pleased to accept your offer of a job at the new Jerusalem Multi-Faith School from September. I am looking forward to working with you.

It would be very useful if some of my future pupils could write me some letters telling me about the plans for the school and about Jerusalem itself. The more they tell me about its history, religion and culture, the better prepared I will be.

Yours sincerely

Sarah Smith

Outcomes By the end of this unit you will:

- understand why Jerusalem means so much to Jews, Christians and Muslims
- explain some similarities and differences in the importance of Jerusalem for these religions
- identify ways of overcoming conflict in a multi-faith school.

Literacy Discuss and share information in groups, draft key points and priorities in preparation for a letter, bring together ideas and information to be put in the letter to the new teacher.

Final task Write a letter to a new teacher at a school in Jerusalem.

Looking ahead to your final task

At the end of this unit you will be replying to this letter. You will find out about Jerusalem. You will write to the new teacher telling her some of the things she needs to know. On each spread you will be prompted to add to your 'Things you need to know' list. How long a letter you write at the end is up to you.

Remember there are already multi-faith schools in Jerusalem but for your task you are creating a new one. So you are not describing a specific school, you are describing your vision – what the ideal multi-faith school should be like.

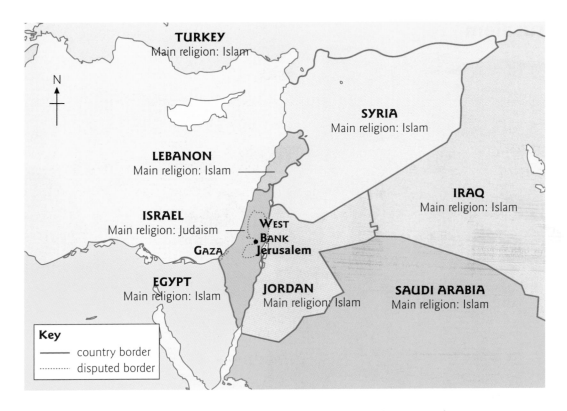

In the noisy, confused maze of the city streets that divide it into four sectors – Jewish, Muslim, Christian and Armenian – nuns, priests, rabbis and imams hurry past each other to fulfil God's work. Each faith has jurisdiction over its own religious sites and at festival times, Jerusalem swells with more devoted pilgrims.

But the city bears the scars of such divisions and heightened atmosphere . . . It is often said that the meaning of the word Jerusalem is the 'city of peace'. If so, the name is an expression of hope rather than any kind of reality.

AA travel guide.

You need to know

- Israel is a small country – about the size of Wales. Population: 6.5 million.
- Population of Jerusalem: 720,000 of whom 70 per cent are Jewish; 30 per cent are Arab (of whom 92 per cent are Muslim and 8 per cent Christian).
- There is an Old City (inside the ancient walls) and a New City outside it. Most of the New City has been built in the last 50 years.
- The Old City has a population of 20,000. The rest live in the New City.
- The Old City is sacred to three monotheistic world faiths – Judaism, Christianity, Islam.
- The Old City is divided into four quarters: Christian, Armenian (a tradition within Christianity), Jewish and Muslim.
- There are no physical barriers (no walls or gates) between the four quarters but they are different in culture and feel.

Task 1

1 Find Israel and Jerusalem on the map. How does Israel compare to surrounding countries:
   a) in size?
   b) in religion?
2 What does the word **monotheist** mean? You can look it up in a dictionary.
3 Now write three bullet points – 'things you need to know' – about **religion** in Jerusalem. Keep your answers. You will add to them as you work through the unit.

Welcome to Jerusalem

A

B

Buskers in the Jewish quarter.

A busy street in the Arab quarter.

C

Boys selling drinks.

D

Jews and Arabs browse a street market.

Palestinian women climb over the wall between Jerusalem and the West Bank.

E

F

Boys selling prayer mats near the Al-Aqsa mosque.

Task 2

For your final task, you will be writing a letter to a new teacher arriving in Jerusalem to teach at your multi-faith school.

Work in pairs. Through this unit you will be thinking about what your new teacher needs to know about Jerusalem and your school.

1 Choose one picture from **A**–**F** above. Imagine yourself or your new teacher standing in this picture. What can you hear? What can you see? What can you smell? What are people thinking? Write down some ideas.
2 Write some bullet points – 'things you need to know' – about **daily life** in Jerusalem.

● What are the three key issues for Jerusalem Multi-Faith School?

The founders of this school want it to help build understanding between the religious groups. They want a school that:

- is open to children from all religions
- respects each child's culture and religion
- helps children to understand and respect others so that they can live alongside each other.

These aims affect every aspect of the school's life but here are three issues that are particularly important. You are an expert in what makes schools work – you've spent nearly ten years in them! What would you do about each issue and why?

Task 3

Work in three groups, taking one issue each, and then report back to the class on your recommendations. Remember your choices must help to further the aims listed here. Issue 1 is simplest, issue 2 is hardest and involves some research.

Issue 1 Code of behaviour

Codes of behaviour help people work together. This is particularly important in a multi-faith school where children come from communities who are in conflict with each other. Write ten rules that you think would help bring harmony in this situation. Here are some ideas to set you thinking.

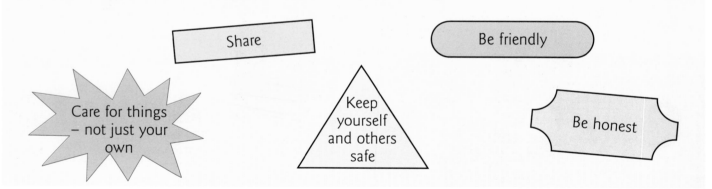

Share

Be friendly

Care for things – not just your own

Keep yourself and others safe

Be honest

Issue 2 School holidays

In schools in the UK the holidays are geared to the Christian calendar. There is a break for Christmas then again for Easter. How would you organise holidays in this multi-faith school in Jerusalem? What are the main festivals for each religion? Remember also that schools often have special events (concerts or assemblies) at festival times. What could be in your plan? You will need to research RE resources at school and in the library as well as websites. Your teacher can give you a sheet to help you as well.

CALENDAR						
1	2	3	4	5	6	7
8	9	10	11	12	13	14
15	16	17	18	19	20	21
22	23	24	25	26	27	28
29	30	31				

Issue 3 Collective worship

The founders want this school to have collective worship. How would you use collective worship to help children understand each other's faiths?

Task 4

1 Look up the word **ethos**. Then write a sentence describing what sort of ethos a multi-faith school should have. Include that in your letter for your final task.
2 Based on what you have decided as a class, add some points to your 'Things you need to know' list (see page 92).

Choice: Separate or together?
Should the children from different religions worship together or separately? Why?

Choice: One religion or many?
Should collective worship focus on one religion at a time or mix them altogether? Why?

Choice: Optional or compulsory?
Should all pupils be forced to go or can they or their parents choose to opt out of collective worship? Why?

Choice: Led by visiting religious leaders or by teachers or by children?
Who is best qualified to lead collective worship? Why?

Choice: Visits to other places of worship or not?
Would regular visits to churches, synagogues or mosques be helpful or unhelpful? Why?

● **What's the history?**

On these pages, you can find out about some of the key moments in Jerusalem's history. Some entries you may recognise from work done in history and RE.

BCE

c. 2000 BCE: The story begins with Abraham who followed God's call. Abraham had two sons: Isaac, son of Sarah (from whom Jews believe they are descended); Ishmael, son of Hagar (from whom Arabs believe they are descended).

Two generations later, the family descended from Isaac went to Egypt to escape famine. In *c.* 1250–1200, Israelites (Jews) escaped from Egypt and re-entered their 'Promised Land', capturing some cities and settling down in others.

In 1000–961 King David captured the city of Jerusalem and made it the capital. His son, Solomon built the very first Temple.

In 587, much of the city and its temple was destroyed by Babylonians and the Jews taken into exile. Fifty years later they were allowed to return and rebuild the ruins. Later, Jerusalem was under Roman rule (from 63 BCE) and the temple that was built by the Jewish king Herod was finally destroyed in 70 CE. The city was in ruins and most Jews fled to other countries.

CE

In the early years of Herod's reign, Jesus of Nazareth was born. He lived for about thirty-three years, spending most of his time in the north of the country but travelling to Jerusalem in the last week of his life. It was in the city that the most important events for Christians took place.

7

In 326 CE, Queen Helena, Christian mother of Emperor Constantine the Great, ordered churches to be built on sites associated with the last week in the life of Jesus, for example, the Church of the Holy Sepulchre (see page 104).

8

In the early seventh century, the new religion of Islam was spreading. The Khaliph Umar entered the city in 638 and the period of Muslim rule began. In 691 the Dome of the Rock was built on the site where Muslims believe Muhammad ﷺ ascended to Heaven and in 715 the Al-Aqsa mosque was erected – the third holiest mosque in Islam.

9

The eleventh and twelfth centuries were the time of the Crusades –'holy wars' – between Christians and Muslims, who fought over the possession of sacred places in and around Jerusalem. The city remained under Muslim rule from 1250 to 1917, first under the Egyptian Marmelukes and then the Ottoman Turks.

10

In the first half of the twentieth century came the rise of Zionism and Anti-Zionism (later developed into the PLO – Palestine Liberation Organisation). During this time (from 1917 to 1948), Britain ruled the country. It promised to set up a national home for Jews.

11

Following the Second World War and the Holocaust, the United Nations voted for a state of Israel to be set up within the borders of Palestine. Arab nations rejected the decision; Jerusalem was divided.

12

In 1967, Arab forces shelled the old city of Jerusalem. The 'Six Day War' followed. Israeli troops captured the old city. Muslims, Christians and Jews were given access to holy places.

The future? However Palestine and Israel settle their political differences, Jerusalem is likely to be one of the most difficult issues to resolve. Your new teacher needs to know some of the history!

Task 5

In your groups (J, C or M) work out historical and religious reasons why Jerusalem is important to you. Write down five key points to include in the letter. Add to your list. You want your new teacher to understand what it is like to be a Jew, Christian or Muslim living in a city of conflict.

13

How does the past affect the present?

PRAYING FOR A MIRACLE

The Sabbath has begun and West Jerusalem has descended into silence.

Somewhere in the distance a dog barks. From elsewhere, far off, a child's voice can be heard.

The smell of cooking wafts throughout the air. Almost every Jewish family will soon be sitting down for their Sabbath dinner. Candles will light up and twinkle through people's windows. The vision of a city at peace with itself.

But across a four-lane road lies another world. East Jerusalem, buzzing with life.

Already a single man's voice has broken the silence. His call, a cry to Allah.

Key

— City Wall
— Western Wall
○ Temple Mount/ al-Haram al-Sharif
☐ Christian Quarter
■ Muslim Quarter
■ Armenian Quarter
☐ Jewish Quarter

DIVIDED CITY

The sound fills every sitting room and kitchen in the West, reminding Jews that they are not alone here in their silence, and with their prayers.

While Jews will pray at their Sabbath dinner for God to help them rebuild Jerusalem, Muslims pray that one day Jerusalem might be theirs again.

All this intensity and Jerusalem is not even a city, really. It's more like a town. And the Old City, encased in the ancient walls, is just one square kilometre of land.

How can such a small piece of land cause so many problems? How can it stop peace in the Middle East?

SO MUCH HATRED

The answer is symbolism. In the Old City, there is the Temple Mount, or the Haram al-Sharif. There, a mosque, which is the third holiest site in Islam, stands almost on top of the Western Wall – one of the holiest sites in Judaism.

Islamic symbolism stands on top of Jewish symbolism. For two peoples between whom there is so much hatred, it's almost too much to bear.

Each side demands sovereignty.

A CITY TO SHARE?

There is a Palestinian in Jerusalem called Abdullah Boudaria, whose house must have one of the most stunning views in the world. It stands literally right opposite the majestic golden dome which symbolises Jerusalem. Pointing to it he told me he lived in the closest place to heaven.

Born in 1922, he has lived through all the turmoil of the city in the twentieth century. He fought in the Arab uprisings against the Jews in the 1930s. He spent seven years hiding from the British, living with the Bedouins. He remembers a night back in 1948 when a huge party was held in Jerusalem. It was the night the UN (United Nations) announced the partition plan which divided Arab and Jew.

Then, one day nineteen years later, he walked into his house and Jerusalem was Arab. When he walked out the next morning, the Jews had taken it over.

Now the 78-year-old has to walk past an Israeli policeman every time he enters or exits his house. He feels humiliated and says his people have lost their dignity.

I asked him this simple question: 'After all these years of trauma, why can't Jew and Arab just live together, share the city?'

He answered emphatically, thrashing the air with his arms: 'We can live together,' he said. 'Back in the Ottoman days there were Arabs, Jews and Christians in this house together. But not now.'

The issue of Jerusalem could scupper a peace deal. And, if so, this would be tragic. The Holy City – oh so holy – could ruin it all.

Adapted from an article by Hilary Andersson for the BBC's 'From our own correspondent'.

Task 6

1 There is a saying about Jerusalem: 'Scratch the present and you'll find the past. Look at the past and you'll see the future.' As a class discuss what this means.
2 Look for examples of this in the report.
3 Discuss this report. Is it neutral or biased (to the Jews, or to the Arabs)? Why do you think this? If you think there is 'loaded language' give examples.
4 It includes an interview with an Arab resident. How might a Jewish resident describe the same events?

Task 7

What key points from these pages would you include in your letter to your teacher? Add at least two points to your list.

For the next three spreads you will work in three groups to concentrate on Judaism, Christianity or Islam.

- The Judaism group will use Task 8 (pages 102–103);
- the Christianity group will use Task 9 (pages 104–105);
- the Muslim group will use Task 10 (pages 106–107).

At the end you will be sharing your information with the other groups to help in their final task.

Each spread deals with some of these aspects:

- sacred writings
- pilgrimage
- place of prayer
- link with history
- focal point for worship

and explains the relevance of Jerusalem for each aspect of each religion.

Why is Jerusalem important to Jews?

Jerusalem is a symbol of Jewish identity – for a person, for a people, through religion and history.

for Judaism group

Sacred writings

*By the rivers of Babylon
there we sat down,
Yea, we wept,
when we remembered Zion [Jerusalem]
. . . If I forget thee, O Jerusalem,
let my right hand forget her cunning.*

From Psalm 137,
written during the Babylonian exile – see page 98.

*David brought up the ark of God . . . into the city
of David . . . set it in the midst of the tabernacle
that David had pitched for it.*

From 2 Samuel 6.

The Ark contained the ten commandments which were placed in the holiest part of the Tabernacle – the special tent that travelled with the ancestors of the Jews when they were in the wilderness after their escape from Egypt.

Later, King David brought the Tabernacle to Jerusalem. His son Solomon built the first Temple to house the sacred Ark. The site is called the Temple Mount.

A place of prayer

When you see the [Western] Wall, you aren't just seeing it with your eyes – there is so much more. There are thousands of years and the weight of millions of Jews there. Your eyes may just see giant bricks and people praying, but your heart sees infinitely more.

At the wall, people pour out their hearts to God, in various languages, at all hours of the day and night. They press messages and prayers (Tzetel) into the cracks that time has worn between the stones. As the story goes, from here, God is a local call. Now, through the internet, people are able to request for their prayers to be offered at the Wall.

The wall is the last remnant of the Temple destroyed by the Romans. Men and women visit separate sections and sightseers remain behind a low barrier. Non-Jews are allowed to go close but men need to cover their heads.

The Western Wall

A link with history – ancient

This tunnel is just one of the many discoveries of archaeologists. It is 530 metres long and was carved out of the rock to bring water from one side of the city to the other. Two crews of diggers started from each end and eventually met in the middle. Because of this water supply, the city did not fall to the Assyrians.

Standing in a rock-hewn tunnel with cold water above my knees, in pitch darkness beneath almost 50 m of bedrock, I feel the wonder, power and drama of Jerusalem more than in almost any other spot. It's those chisel marks that do it, scored across the walls in parallel rows . . . as sharp and fresh as they were when carved by King Hezekiah's men 2,700 years ago. [See 2 Chronicles 32.30.]

Adapted from the *Jerusalem Post*.

Hezekiah's tunnel

A link with history – recent

Yad Vashem means 'memorial and a name' (for every victim of the Holocaust).

For anyone who has come to Israel to gain understanding of the Jews and their land, a morning at Yad Vashem is essential.

From a non-Jewish travel guide.

The children's memorial has a light for every one of the 1.5 million children and babies killed. Their names, places of birth and ages are read out continuously.

Yad Vashem

A focal point for worship

For over two thousand years, since the destruction of the Temple, the Western Wall in Jerusalem has been the Jewish focal point for prayer. When Jews pray, no matter where they are, they face in its direction.

Task 8

1 Which examples would you most want the new teacher to know about and understand? Make a top three priority list, giving reasons for your choice.
2 Draft a paragraph for the letter which explains your feelings about Jerusalem as a Jew.

● **Why is Jerusalem important to Christians?**

for
Christianity
group

Christianity grew out of Judaism. Jesus was a Jew, as were many of his first followers.

The Jewish Bible forms part of the Christian Bible (the Old Testament) and so many of the Biblical events shown on pages 98–99 are also the background to the story of Christianity.

Jesus actually spent very little time in Jerusalem. He was brought to the temple as a baby and came on Jewish pilgrimage when he was twelve.

It is the momentous events of the last week in his life, Holy Week, that make the city so important to Christians. It is what makes Jerusalem a centre of Christian pilgrimage.

Church of the Holy Sepulchre

The Tomb

The Hill of the Skull

The Garden Tomb

A link with history and a place of pilgrimage

The Church of the Holy Sepulchre is located in the centre of the Christian quarter of the city. It was first identified as the place of Jesus' death and resurrection by the Christian mother of Emperor Constantine. The church as it is now was mainly built at the time of the Crusades.

Inside the church there is a rocky outcrop which is believed to be the place where Jesus was crucified. Archaeologists confirm that this would have been outside the city walls at that time.

The first-century tombs inside the church show that the site could have been the location of the tomb given by Joseph of Arimathea for the burial of Jesus.

In 1884, the British General Gordon noticed a skull-like rocky outcrop (known as the Hill of the Skull) and proposed that this was the site of the crucifixion. He believed it possible that an ancient tomb (the Garden Tomb) found close by could be the tomb in which Jesus was placed.

Which is the place where Jesus died and rose again?

Both places are visited by pilgrims today. Some Christians prefer the Hill of the Skull/Garden Tomb to the Church of the Holy Sepulchre as this church is rather gloomy with lots of elaborate decoration, candles and incense. Archaeologists favour the Church of the Holy Sepulchre as the most likely location of these important events.

For all Christians, it is what they believe about the events of the crucifixion and resurrection that is important.

A place for prayer

During Holy Week, Christians walk the way of the cross (the Via Dolorosa), stopping at various points to pray. Some of these stopping points are in the Bible, some are traditional.

And after that they had mocked him, they took the robe off from him, and put his own raiment upon him and led him away to crucify him. And as they came out, they found a man of Cyrene, Simon by name; they compelled him to bear his cross.

And when they were come to the place of Golgotha, that is to say, the place of a skull, they gave him vinegar to drink . . . And they crucified him and parted his garments, casting lots.

From Matthew 27.31–35.

The Via Dolorosa

A focal point for worship

Traditionally, church altars face East, the direction of Jerusalem in the Holy Land and the sites of the crucifixion and resurrection.

Task 9

1 Which examples would you most want the new teacher to know about and understand? Make a top three priority list, giving reasons for your choice.
2 Draft a paragraph for the letter which explains your feelings about Jerusalem as a Christian.

● Why is Jerusalem important to Muslims?

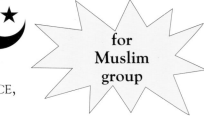

for Muslim group

'Islam' means peace brought about by obedience to Allah. A 'Muslim' is one who accepts the teaching that 'There is no God except Allah, Muhammad ﷺ is the messenger of Allah'.

The prophet Muhammad ﷺ was born in 570 CE. Beginning in 610 CE, he had a series of visions which convinced him that Allah had a final message for the world.

The sacred writings and prophets of Judaism and Christianity (including Abraham, David and Jesus) had revealed the message of Allah (God). Now, there was a new and final revelation from Allah.

Muhammad ﷺ was the 'mouthpiece' for this new message. Recited by him and then recorded, it became the Qur'an – the sacred writing of Islam.

The message soon spread and Islam grew rapidly. A few years after Muhammad's ﷺ death in 632 CE, Muslim forces reached Palestine and Jerusalem was handed over after a brief siege.

The Temple Mount is known to Muslims as 'The Noble Sanctuary' (Al-Haram al-Sharif).

In area, the Noble Sanctuary covers nearly one-sixth of the old walled city of Jerusalem. The whole area is regarded as a mosque. It consists of 35 acres (over 14 square kilometres) of fountains, gardens, buildings and domes. At the southern end, there is the Al-Aqsa mosque. In the centre is the Dome of the Rock.

Sacred writings

Glorified be he Who carried His servant by night... to the Far Distant Place of Worship, the neighbourhood whereof We have blessed.
    Qur'an, Sura 17. Muslims believe that the Temple Mount was this 'Far Distant Place'. It is one of the three most important sites in Islam.

Link with history and a place of pilgrimage

Dome of the Rock

The Dome of the Rock is in the centre of the Noble Sanctuary. It was built in 688–691 CE by Abd el-Malik. Inside, under the dome, is a black rock. There is a tradition that, from this rock, Muhammad ﷺ made a night time journey to heaven on a winged horse, with the Angel Gabriel.

Also inside the Dome is this inscription:
O you People of the Book, overstep not bounds in your religion, and of God speak only the truth. The Messiah, Jesus, son of Mary, is only an apostle of God, and his Word, which he conveyed unto Mary, and a Spirit proceeding from him. Believe therefore in God and his apostles, and say not Three. It will be better for you. God is only one God. Far be it from his glory that he should have a son.

Al-Aqsa mosque

In 638 CE, following the siege, the Khaliph Umar entered Jerusalem on foot. Umar asked to be taken to the site of the Al-Aqsa mosque. Accompanied by hundreds of Muslims, he found the area covered in dust and debris and immediately initiated its clearing. A huge timber mosque which held three thousand worshippers was erected on this site in the time of Umar.

The Al-Aqsa mosque, restored in 1948.

Task 10

1 Which examples would you most want the new teacher to know about and understand? Make a top three priority list, giving reasons for your choice.
2 Draft a paragraph for the letter which explains your feelings about Jerusalem as a Muslim.

● How does a multi-faith school work?

Yours is a new multi-faith school. But there is already one in existence.

Case study: Neve Shalom – Wahut al-Salam

The school takes its name from the village in which it was started. NEVE SHALOM and WAHUT AL-SALAM both mean 'oasis of peace'. The village was founded by a Christian monk in 1972. He believed that peace, respect and co-existence was possible between people of different cultures and religions. The Jews and Palestinian Arabs who came to live in the village believed that too.

One of the first things they did was to start a school – a school for peace.

That was over thirty years ago. Today this village school receives 90 per cent of its children from other Arab and Jewish communities. The village also works with adults from other communities to pass on their experience and to bring about more reconciliation between Arab and Jew.

These are the ways it has put those beliefs about peace, respect and co-existence into practice:

1 Equality between Jews and Palestinians in management and teaching in the school
2 Children have many opportunities to work and play with each other
3 Hebrew (the language of the Jews) and Arabic (the language of the Arabs) are both used in the teaching
4 The culture and religion of all the children is respected and they are taught to respect the culture and religion of others.

A special event: celebration of Ramadan, Hannukah and Christmas

The learning process that led up to today was rich, educational and moving for all of us – grown-ups and children alike. We had an opportunity to learn about ourselves and about each other's cultures.

The staff and the children . . . prepared materials, information, activities and music. The main display was an exhibition of art related to the festivals. There was music and singing, quizzes and board games, all based on the festivals.

Another similar event was organised around the festivals of New Higra Year of Islam, the Jewish Passover and the Christian Easter festival.
Weeks of hard work by the children and teachers had been put into this event. The outcome was very moving. It was a pleasure to see the children teaching their parents the stories of the other religions. It was exciting to see the people standing there, reading together, exchanging impressions.

The event filled us with hope, touching upon the possibility that we shall yet reach the times when our two peoples will contribute to each other and enrich one another, instead of hating and killing one another.

From the school's website.

Quotes from letters of thanks from Jewish, Muslim and Christian parents

Congratulations on your activity, which gives hope and light in these dark days. The exhibition you created is very impressive and moving and I have learned new things.

The event was very beautiful and enabled us to learn about the Higra New Year and about Easter, things that we have not known.

The essence of this event is love, acceptance and an act of giving to all religions. If only there were understanding and love and peace in our country as those we experience here.

Task 11

1 List three main ideas from Neve Shalom which you think would help understanding and co-operation in a multi-faith school. Make a chart like this:

Ideas and activities	Intended outcome
Use Hebrew and Arabic for teaching	Children will be able to communicate with each other

2 What will you tell the new teacher about this school?

Final task

So . . . what are you going to tell your new teacher about your school and about Jerusalem?

Prepare to write a welcoming letter to a new teacher coming from England to a multi-faith school in Jerusalem. This teacher has not visited Jerusalem before and has asked for help from you!

In this unit, you have found out some of the things that make Jerusalem so special – its history, politics and places of religious importance. You have seen how one multi-faith school works. You have prepared some ideas for your own! You need to bring those ideas together in a personal letter.

1 As a group:

- share and explain your draft paragraphs about your three Jewish or Christian or Muslim priorities
- find the answers to the questions below. You might decide to tell the teacher about them.

a) What do Christians and Jews have in common about the importance of Jerusalem? What differences? (see pages 98–99 and 102–105)
b) What does the inscription in the Dome of the Rock tell you about the similarities and differences between Muslims and Christians in their beliefs about God and Jesus? (see page 107)
c) Why is the Temple Mount likely to be a cause of conflict between Jews and Muslims? (see page 100)

2 On your own:

- look back at Tasks 1–7 (Your 'Things you should know' lists)
- make sure you have a copy of the two other draft paragraphs about religious priorities
- plan your letter.

Your letter

Jerusalem, _____ 20 _____

Dear Teacher

I am looking forward to welcoming you here and I am looking forward to being taught by you.

I am writing to tell you some things about our school and the city of Jerusalem.

There are many things that make our school special. These are some of them:

_____

_____

I hope you will agree that our school is special. If I had to sum up the ethos of our school, I would say: _____

_____

Of course I am sure you will have heard of the conflicts that we have in this city and it is important that you know about some of them before you come.

_____

_____

In our school there are students from three religions.
I am a _____. This is why the city is important to me:

_____

_____

In my class there are also _____ and _____.

The city is important to the _____ because

It is also important to the _____ because

I hope you will like it here in Jerusalem. We are all looking forward to meeting you.

Best wishes

8 Technology – beauty or beast?

Outcomes By the end of this unit you will:

- understand how gene technology could change our future
- evaluate some benefits and dangers of technology
- identify issues that technology could raise for religion.

Literacy Discuss in groups, draft guidelines using information from the unit, sort information found, compile two sets of commandments, explain the results.

Final task Compile two sets of commandments for people in their exercise of power over technology.

Looking ahead to your final task

Improvements in technology have given humans greater power than ever before. How we use that technology is up to us. We could make technology into a beauty or a beast. In this unit you will be writing ten new commandments specifically to guide the use of technology: to make it a beauty, not a beast. You will start by looking at one aspect of technology: GENE TECHNOLOGY. Then widen it out.

GENES INC OFFERS YOU THE CHANCE OF A LIFETIME!

We can reprogramme your genes to make your perfect human being!
You have to decide what is perfect.

Start creating!
Listed below are twenty genes you can purchase from Genes Inc.
You can choose up to five. Just tick the ones you want.

Health Good health	☐
Relationships Out with friends every night	☐
Intellectual ability Good general knowledge (e.g. good at quizzes)	☐
Get good results in exams	☐
Enjoy solving problems (e.g. chess, computer games)	☐
Practical skills Ability to read and write	☐
Sporting skills, such as being good at ball games	☐
Creative skills such as drawing or playing music	☐
Beliefs A belief in God	☐
Knowing the difference between right and wrong	☐
A belief in life after death	☐
Values Rich countries should share with poor	☐
Democracy and equal opportunities	☐
Desire for great personal wealth (e.g. winning the Lottery)	☐
Personal characteristics Generous and unselfish	☐
Good sense of humour	☐
Hard working	☐
Physical characteristics Taller or shorter than I am now	☐
Different hair/eye colour	☐
Attractive to the opposite sex	☐
Total	☐

Task 1

1 Look at the form above. On your own copy, mark the five genes you want to buy. You will have to make some hard choices. You can amend the list by adding up to five genes of your choice which are not already included.
2 Explain why such a collection of genes would make you into a successful human being.
3 Discuss: If this were really possible would that be good or bad? Why?

● Gene technology: what is possible now?

On Jeans for Genes day, many schools raise funds for medical research into gene therapy. What do you know about genes and what is happening in the research?

Maybe the ideas on pages 112–113 seemed far-fetched to you. But what **is** possible now?

These two pages explain the current state of developments in gene technology. But read closely: we have added one false story. Can you spot it?

Gene therapy

This is to treat inherited diseases caused by faulty genes. It will soon be possible to replace or repair the faulty genes. Doctors extract bone marrow, insert healthy genes into some of the bone marrow cells and then transfuse it back into the patient. In the picture, a scientist is adding a corrective, healthy gene to a faulty immune system.

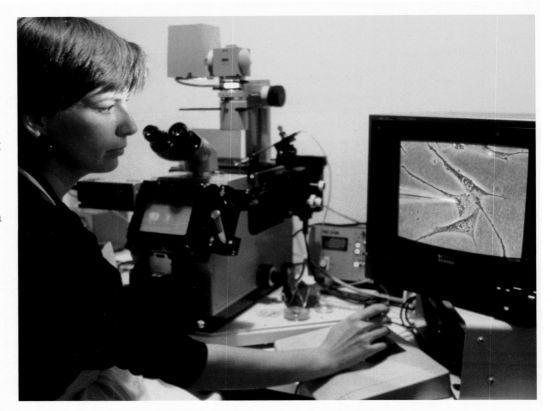

The treatment is at a very early stage. There have been some successes. For example, a two-year-old boy has been successfully treated at Great Ormond Street Hospital for an inherited disease which meant he had no immune system. He had to be totally isolated from the world – he was a 'baby in a bubble'.

Genetic screening

This is for couples who run the risk of passing on genetic diseases to their children such as haemophilia and cystic fibrosis. The EMBRYOS can be removed and screened in the laboratory for the infected genes. Only unaffected embryos will be put back in the mother's womb. The others will be discarded.

Using genes to change skin colour

It has been possible for over a decade to affect the skin colour of a baby. For example, by 1993 Italian doctors had implanted a fertilised egg, donated by a white woman, into the womb of a black woman. So, prospective parents could choose the skin colour and racial grouping of their offspring.

Genetic engineering and modification

Scientists can now alter the genes of any living thing – plants (for example, crops which are genetically modified to resist disease), animals and human beings. They can create new kinds of plants or animals by changing or engineering their genetic make-up, for example, by using human genes. This cress has had the genes from another plant introduced to make it grow better, or faster or greener.

Gene bank

These test tubes contain the entire human genome in one fridge. Each tube contains one particular region of DNA, responsible for one aspect of human life.

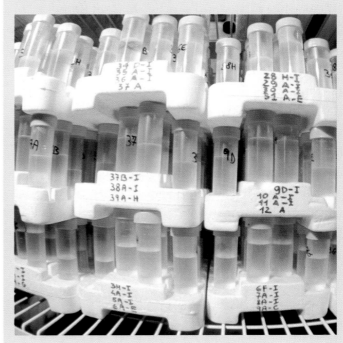

Genes and your personality

It is now possible to modify genes in order to create people of superior intelligence, perfect weight and happy personalities. Your surroundings, wealth, education and diet can all be overcome if you are created with the right combination of genes in the laboratory. Environment and upbringing do not matter.

Task 2

1 Which is the deliberate mistake?
2 With a partner, write down three benefits ('beauties') of genetic technology.
3 Write one or more guidelines for management of genetic technology. These will help towards your final task.

● A perfect baby – a look into the future

This story reflects on what gene technology has been able to do already and what it might do in the future!

For Trevor and Tracy, it was the moment every parent finds difficult. Sharon, their eldest, had started asking The Question: where did I come from, Mummy? As she patted her daughter's blond hair (catalogue number: HC 205) and looked into her perfect cornflower blue eyes (EC 317), Tracy decided that, in 2095, there was nothing to be squeamish about. She began to explain to Sharon, who had heard disturbing rumours about how in the old days, when a man and a woman wanted to have a baby, they went to bed with each other and left the outcome to passion and chance. Well, this was not the way her father and mother had set about bringing their daughter into the world, Tracy assured her.

It was virtually inconceivable that any responsible parent could permit a child to be born whose genes had been left to the chance shuffling of natural processes, although there were rumours of underground groups that still practised 'chance childbirth' as it was called. No, that was quite obscene. No parent would allow a foetus to go through nine months of development without knowing the colour of its eyes, or whether it had

Your father is at work

straight hair or wavy. Good grief, no one would ever conceive a child without specifying the genes for its intelligence quotient, which would help determine its chances in education and subsequent employment.

No, Sharon had to understand that Trevor and Tracy had been thorough. They had gone to the Ideal Baby exhibition at Olympia and they had combed through months of back issues of *Genes and Babies* magazine. They had window-shopped hopefully at the Harrods' Baby Counter (but the prices were prohibitive).

Tracy's job was not well paid and there had been a recession at the genetically engineered food factory where Trevor worked so, Tracy reflected, it might be better not to mention the fact that they had not been able to afford the most expensive high intelligence genetic profile for Sharon.

They had settled for a cheaper model (catalogue number: IQ 200). Sharon would therefore always be less intelligent than her schoolfriend Charlotte, whose grandparents had taken out a second mortgage to help purchase for her the genes guaranteeing ultra-high intelligence (catalogue number: IQ 300).

At that point Trevor returned from work. As she saw him Tracy felt, as always, joy that he was still alive. In an unpleasant incident at work involving the plutonium and the cobalt-60 source of gamma rays, Trevor's spleen, liver and kidneys had been destroyed. But the two of them were fortunate that they had taken out extra health insurance to cover genetic engineering of a pig, which was bred to provide organs suitable for transplant and which were virtually guaranteed not to be rejected by Trevor's immune system.

As Sharon listened, she became impatient. 'All very interesting,' she said, wriggling on the sofa, 'but *Neighbours* will be on in a minute, can't you just tell me where I came from?' Tracy wondered why they hadn't spent a bit more money to get one of the higher-powered patience genes that had just come on the market, so she finished her story.

By the middle of the 21st century, advances in science had produced female gorillas with a virtually human reproductive system. So a human egg fertilised *in vitro* could be implanted in the uterus of such a gorilla. That was how Sharon had been born.

After Tracy and Trevor had chosen her genes, they had come back to Genes 'R' Us nine months later to pick up their new child which had been nurtured in the surrogate womb of a genetically engineered female gorilla. Tracy, happily, was spared the bother and inconvenience of having to be pregnant, and the difficulties and pain of birth.

Adapted from an article in *The Independent* by Tom Wilkie.

Task 3

Read the story carefully then first of all have some fun with it.

1 In small groups choose one of the following scenarios and role-play what happens.

- Sharon complains to Trevor and Tracy that she doesn't like the hair they chose for her.
- Trevor and Tracy visit the boss of the gene company to ask for their money back because Sharon has grown up to be a bolshy teenager.
- Sharon tells Trevor and Tracy she and her boyfriend Daniel will practise 'chance childbirth' if they ever have children.
- Charlotte and Sharon bring home their GCSE results.

2 Of course in the UK at the moment all this is impossible. If any of it were possible it would certainly be illegal. But this is supposed to be a fable or a moral tale. It is a fantasy but it still has meaning for the real world. It has various warnings. For example:

a) about pushy parents
b) about the false appeal of perfection
c) about what happens when human life becomes a commodity to buy and sell.

Explain one of these warnings in your own words. Keep this. It will be useful for your final task.

● Born for a purpose: to help my brother

In 2001 a British woman gave birth to a baby genetically designed to provide tissue that could help her then four-year-old son in his battle against leukaemia. She had travelled to Chicago to take advantage of technology that is not currently available or allowed in the UK.

The doctor takes embryos grown in the laboratory at the eight-cell stage and takes a cell biopsy, screening them for genetic abnormalities. He then implants only a healthy embryo to ensure it will be a good, healthy bone marrow match.

The child was the first in the UK to have been created in such a way. The woman's elder son is recovering from leukaemia. However, there is a one in four chance of a relapse. If that happens, the boy will need a bone marrow transplant. A brother or sister created to have an immune system which is a perfect match will give a transplant operation the best possible chance of success.

● Born for a purpose: to fit well with my family

A lesbian couple in the United States, both of whom are deaf, deliberately chose to have a deaf child by selecting a sperm donor who was also deaf. They were successful and now have two deaf children.

Task 4

1 Discuss in groups: What is similar about these case studies? What is different?
2 Is one of them more acceptable to you than the other? If so, which one and why?
3 On the facing page are a range of statements generated by the controversy surrounding these and similar cases.
   Sort these statements into 'beauty' (this technology is a help to humankind) and 'beast' (this technology is harmful). Some will be easier than others.
4 Go back to question 2. Do you want to change your answer?

You need to know

- In the UK, the Human Fertilisation and Embryology Authority (HFEA) has to give permission for new ways of using technology like this. It did not give permission in the leukaemia case – that's why the parents went abroad.
- In law, experiments on embryos can be carried out in the first fourteen days of 'life'.

A

All these ETHICAL dilemmas are very easy when you haven't been put on the spot yourself. At least we can look each other in the eye and say there was something out there that could be done and we did it.
Parents

B

There might be problems in the future for the new baby. We have to think about that, not just the needs of the brother. What if something goes wrong?
Children's worker

C

Is the child being born for its own sake or for someone else's?
HFEA (see panel opposite)

D

We are not creating designer babies. We are not trying to choose eye colour or hair colour. We are trying to prevent an illness.
Doctor

E

Once you have allowed couples to have a choice over what their baby is like, it is not possible to attack the choices people then make. Once you have started interfering in the natural process, then different people's ideas of normality are going to have to be considered. Deaf people consider they are just living a different normality.
Spokesman for a medical ethics organisation

F

What many hearing people do not understand is that many deaf people are happy to be deaf. . . . There are deaf parents who welcome the fact that their baby is born deaf, therefore allowing them to share their cultural identity and language.
Spokesman for the British Deaf Association

G

Children should not be created to serve the needs of the parents. Children should be loved and accepted unconditionally. This child was born on the condition that he was deaf.
Spokesman for LIFE organisation

H

I think all of us recognise that deaf children have perfectly wonderful lives. The question is whether the parents have violated the sacred duty of parenthood, which is to maximise to some reasonable degree the advantages available to their children.
Professor of law and bioethics

I

A number of rabbis believe that since the purpose [of genetic engineering in the case of an incurable illness] is to heal, it is fulfilling the task that God has imposed upon doctors. This only allows genetic manipulation to heal the sick, it doesn't permit the right to choose eye colour or other features.
Jewish website

J

I do fear for the future . . . if the language of bodily human love is gradually replaced by an artificial process, if procreation becomes production or even reproduction, and if the individual human being becomes valued as a product to be ordered rather than a gift to be received.
The late Cardinal Basil Hume, in an article in *The Independent*, 15 March 1997

Task 5

1 Which of the following groups might welcome developments in gene technology?
   a) A commercial company with money to spend on genetic research.
   b) A religious group that believes that the birth of a child is a gift from God.
   c) A government who wants to ensure a harmonious and peaceful society.
2 Working on your own, use all the information and tasks from this unit so far to help you begin to draft your ten commandments for the future management of gene technology. This will help towards your final task.

Twenty-first-century technology – beauty or beast?

So far you have only been investigating one aspect of technology – gene technology. Now you are going to widen your view.

On these pages are some technological advances of the last hundred years. You need to decide how this technology has been harmful or beneficial for human life and nature on this planet.

2 mobile phone

I computers and the internet

3 car

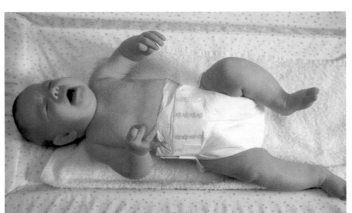

4 disposable nappies

5 space exploration

6 TV

7 nuclear power

8 fast food packaging

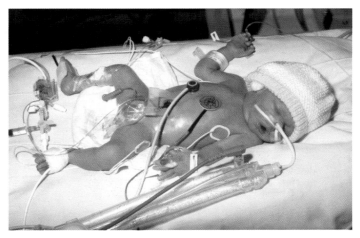

9 intensive care for premature babies

10 guided missiles

Task 6

Working in pairs, decide whether each invention (**1–10**) is a beauty or a beast.

- If it is a beauty, without doubt, it is something which has brought mainly benefits for human beings.
- If it is a beast, without doubt, it is something which has brought mainly disasters for human beings.
- Or, if it is both, it has brought both benefits and disasters. In each case, identify why.

Use a chart like this to record your views.

Technological advance	Beauty?	Beast?	Both?	Why?
computers and the internet				
mobile phone				
car				
disposable nappies				
space exploration				
TV				
nuclear power				
fast food packaging				
intensive care				
guided missiles				

What guidance do religions give about technology?

For your final task you will be writing ten commandments for the use of technology. Your commandments are going to include five religious ones. This spread helps you with these.

Because sacred writings were formed centuries ago, they do not say anything specific about technology. People have to apply the basic values and teachings of those writings to modern dilemmas. They will also follow the advice of modern religious teachers.

For example:

1 Seek wisdom and understanding.

2 Do not worship false gods.

3 Do not try to become equal with God.

4 Allow for human nature.

5 Do not work all the time.

6 Do not kill.

7 Do not steal.

8 Do not lie.

9 Do not envy.

10 Love one another.

11 Look after the environment.

12 Understand God's purpose.

13 Help the poor.

14 Have good intentions.

15 Live simply.

Task 7

Statements 1–15 are commandments, ideas or principles from different religious traditions. They are general. Your task is to apply them to the use of technology.

1 Working in pairs make a table like this and fill it out for as many statements as you can.

Statement	Application to the use of technology
Do not kill	Use technology to preserve life not to bring death.
Do not worship false gods	Don't let technology take over your life. Keep it in perspective.

NB You probably won't be able to do them all. Some are trickier than others.

2 From your completed table, highlight up to five statements in the second column that you think are particularly important. They may be useful for your final task.

Beauty or beast?

There are some religious groups who believe that particular forms of technology, for example, computers and television/film, are evil. These religious groups believe it is better to protect themselves and their children from such influences altogether.

Chasidic Jews, for example, are Orthodox Jews who try to keep themselves separate from society. They dress traditionally, have separate schools, and don't take jobs that would require them to compromise. As far as technology goes they don't have televisions because it would invite the corrupting influence of the outside world into their homes.

However, the vast majority of religious people are neutral on the subject of technology, because technology is morally neutral. They say it is the impact and use of technology in human hands that makes a difference. Where technology has a positive impact on the quality of human life and reveals more about God's world, technology is good. Where it harms people, or distracts worshippers from God, or destroys the environment, technology is bad.

Gandhi

Mahatma Gandhi lived a famously technology-free life. He deliberately chose to live amongst the outcasts to show how much they should be valued. He taught that the duty of a Hindu was to relieve the suffering of others. As a Hindu, he believed in the sacredness of all life and in non-violence. He had a great respect for the natural world.

He resisted the advances of technology in the woollen mills of England because it deprived Indian workers of a living and caused them to suffer. However, he also knew the power of the media and was happy to use it if it supported his aim to free India from British rule.

Task 8

1 Look back at the religious values/teachings on page 122. Apply these teachings to three of the examples on pages 120–121. For example, space exploration teaches us more about our galaxy, but does use up financial resources that could be otherwise used to improve life for the poor on Earth.
2 Use your answers to the questions above to help you prepare for writing your five religious commandments in your final task.

Preparing for your final task: some reminders

In the future, humans could have the power to design and create a life which matches their idea of perfection, such as the one you planned on page 113 or the one Tracy and Trevor bought for Sharon!

Religions have to apply their values/teachings to the use of technology.

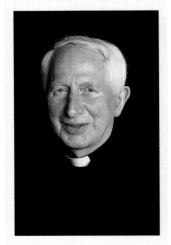

Technology transforms the media and our ability to communicate – it doesn't mean we will say the right things.

There is a difference between being powerful and being wise,

Technology is morally neutral until it is in the hands of human beings, who can make crucial decisions about its use to save or destroy life.

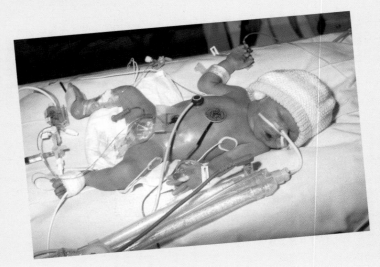

Final task

Compile two sets of commandments so that, in the future, technology becomes 'beauty' and not 'beast'.

Preparation

Look back at each section of the unit and the work you have done. You should have already drafted some commandments. Redraft those or write some now.

1 Examine them carefully and discuss with others. Ask 'How will this make the future better?'
2 Divide your commandments into secular and religious. This may take some time. If you don't have enough in either category, think about how you could rewrite them. For secular, look particularly at pages 114–115; for religious, look particularly at pages 122–123.

Writing

Now it is time to draw up your final set.

3 Record your commandments on tablets like this.

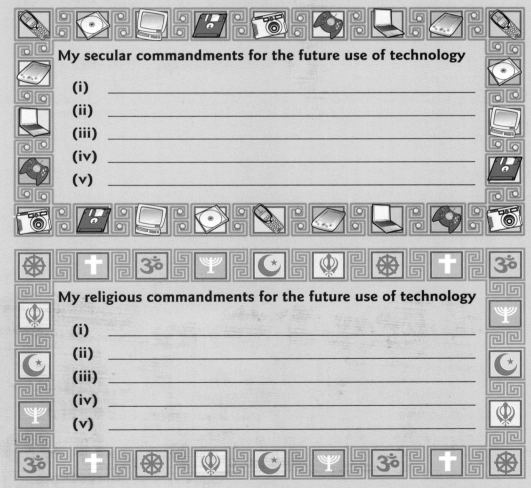

My secular commandments for the future use of technology

(i) _____

(ii) _____

(iii) _____

(iv) _____

(v) _____

My religious commandments for the future use of technology

(i) _____

(ii) _____

(iii) _____

(iv) _____

(v) _____

4 Choose one commandment from each set that you think is the most likely to make technology a 'beauty' and not a 'beast'. Explain your choice.

9 Bridges and barriers

Task 1

Discuss:
1 Which bridge do you like best?
2 Which would you least like to cross?
3 Which one will last the longest?
4 Which do you think cost the most to build?
5 Which is the oldest?
6 Which could the world do without?

A

San Francisco

B

The border crossing between Zaire and Rwanda

C Venice

D The Lake District

E Malaysia

F Castle of Romena, Italy

Task 2

The bridges are very different but they have something in common. Each has a barrier to cross. Without a barrier, there is no need for a bridge. You are going to use this idea as a way of thinking about your life, the world and religion, looking for symbolic bridges and barriers.

1 Think about phrases using 'bridge' in a symbolic way, for example, 'building bridges' and 'bridging the gap'.
  a) Give an example of a real life situation where one of these phrases might apply.
  b) The title of a once-popular song, 'Bridge over troubled water', uses the idea of a bridge in another way. The singer offers to be a 'bridge over troubled water'. What might this mean? Your teacher can tell you more.
2 Start a list of ideas for your final task: ways of 'bridging'; different sorts of barriers.

● The Mostar story

THE BOSNIAN WAR claimed another

priceless architectural treasure yesterday

when the old Turkish bridge spanning the river Neretva at Mostar, and for centuries linking the Catholic lands to the West with the Muslim interior, finally collapsed under the pressure of Croatian shells.

Built in 1566, the steep-backed, high-arched bridge had withstood eighteen months of Serbian and Croatian onslaught, latterly bedecked with a necklace of rubber tyres placed there by the besieged Muslim community in an attempt to bolster it.

Yesterday morning it gave way. The bridge was a powerful symbol of cross-cultural links and inter-ethnic tolerance.

The name Mostar comes from Stari Most – old bridge. It was Mostar's main attraction before the war.

Urchins would solicit money by diving from it.

The old Turkish quarter edging the bridge, a warren of coffee shops, silversmiths, tailors and milliners, was battered by Serbian shells early in the war, and has been reduced to rubble by the Croats pounding the East bank of the river where some 50,000 Muslims are holed up.

Before the war, Mostar was evenly split between Muslims and Croats. But the Croats claimed it as their capital.

Adapted from an article in *The Guardian*, November 1993.

The Mostar bridge three months later.

Building a new bridge or 'building bridges'?

The bridge crossed the River Neretva. But it also united Christian and Muslim territory. So when the war ended and the bridge was rebuilt, this was a symbolic moment.

We, the men, used to show our bravery to our fiancées by jumping in the river from the deck of the bridge before getting married. This did not belong to a specific ethnic group. It was a common tradition.
Mostar inhabitant.

The famous sixteenth-century bridge of Mostar is being re-constructed. Some parts of the bridge rescued from the river are being used to rebuild the stone span.

   The rebuilding of the structure is meant to symbolise reunification and is a crucial step in the healing process of the ethnically-divided town of Mostar, which was devastated by the war.

   Project head, Rusmir Cisic told the news agency, 'We do not want the bridge only to link two sides of a river like bridges usually do. We want to link peoples in Mostar, which after the conflict remained one of the most destroyed cities in Europe.

From the BBC news website, June 2001.

Task 3

1 In what ways could the Mostar bridge story be described as a death and a resurrection?
2 Write a paragraph about the rebuilding of the Mostar bridge as if for a feature on *Newsround*, making sure you explain how the bridge is a symbol. You could do some research on http://www.nato.int/sfor/engineers/mostarbridge/mostar.htm
3 Sketch some images from these pages that you might use in your final task.

● Why is Corrymeela a bridge?

Corrymeela is a 'bridge' between two communities who have been in conflict with each other for many years – Catholics and PROTESTANTS in Northern Ireland.

Corrymeela means 'the hill of harmony'. It is the name given to premises in Northern Ireland first purchased in the 1960s by the Rev. Ray Davey. He had been captured in Germany during the Second World War and witnessed the allied bombing of Dresden when many civilians died. He wanted to help bring reconciliation and healing to troubled communities. On his return to Northern Ireland, he set up the Corrymeela community.

These are some of the things they do:

CORRYMEELA *IS* PEOPLE OF ALL AGES AND CHRISTIAN TRADITIONS, WHO, INDIVIDUALLY AND TOGETHER ARE COMMITTED TO THE HEALING OF SOCIAL, RELIGIOUS & POLITICAL DIVISIONS THAT EXIST IN NORTHERN IRELAND AND THROUGHOUT THE WORLD

- Residential projects for schools, twinned Protestant and Catholic
- Training programme for teenagers on racism, sectarianism and discrimination
- Support for projects working for peace and reconciliation
- Training for people working to help in places of conflict, not just in Northern Ireland
- Sanctuary for victims of stress
- Children's bereavement service

'I learnt that people on the other side are just like me.'
Corrymeela is a pretty cool place. Catholic and Protestant children can get on together and learn about each other there. In Northern Ireland there has been a lot of fighting and disagreements between people and this means that children of different beliefs don't often get the chance to meet, as most of them go to separate schools and live in separate areas.

At Corrymeela children can share their own stories and experiences as well as have a good time together.

From www.globalgang.org.uk.

Final task

So . . . what are the bridges and barriers in life and religion?

Your challenge and your final task in this course is to create a 3D model or a computer graphic of a bridge, overcoming a barrier of some sort. You also need to create a commentary to explain it.

Your graphic should sum up something significant you have learned from this course. You might feel that this course has taught you something interesting or useful about religion. So your barrier could be your own disinterest and your bridge could be your teacher.

But that might be a bit creepy! So here are some other examples:

An example from your own life
You might feel you face many barriers in your own life between what you want to be and what you are. We looked at these ideas in Unit 1. So your barrier could be the fences that surround you; and the bridge could be some guidance that helps you overcome them.

An example from religion
We looked at suffering in Unit 5. You might feel that suffering in the world is a barrier between you and God or between other people and God. So your barrier could be suffering in the world; your bridge could be Rosalind Grimshaw's story overcoming suffering and celebrating creation.

An example from the modern world
We looked at Jerusalem in Unit 7. You might feel that mistrust between different religious or ethnic groups is a barrier to peace. So your barrier could be the history that fuels that mistrust; your bridge could be a multi-faith school such as Neve Shalom that encourages different religious groups to try to understand each other.

These are just examples. What you choose and how you present it is up to you.

Glossary

AGNOSTIC   A person who doubts, or who has yet to be convinced, that there is a God

AKHIRAH   In Islam, everlasting life after death

ATHEIST   A person who does not believe in the existence of God

BAR MITZVAH   Means 'Son of Commandment' – a Jewish boy's coming of age at 13 years old, usually marked by a synagogue ceremony and family celebration

BARZAKH   In Islam, a time of waiting for judgement for those who have already died

BET CHAYIM   A name given to a Jewish cemetery, meaning 'house of life'

BHAVACHAKRA   Buddhist wheel of life (bhava – becoming, chakra – wheel)

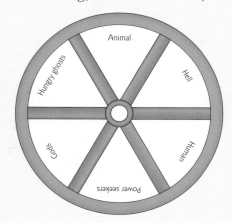

CATHOLIC   In Christianity, often used as an abbreviation for Roman Catholic

CIRCUMCISION   Cutting off the foreskin of the penis of Jewish boys as a religious rite, usually on the eighth day after birth

CREATION   The beginning of the natural world, as in creation stories

EIGHTFOLD PATH   The Buddha's teaching on the way to live, such as Perfect Speech, Perfect Action and Perfect Effort

EMBRYO   The human product of conception in the early days of pregnancy

ETHICAL   In accordance with moral values

EUCHARIST   Means 'thanksgiving'. The name given to a service celebrating the resurrection of Jesus Christ, using bread and wine. Also known as Holy Communion

EVOLUTION   Gradual change in species over time, according to Darwin's theory

FAITH   Strong belief which does not rely on proof, for example, religious faith

GENE TECHNOLOGY   The application of scientific/medical knowledge and skill to human reproduction, especially that which affects heredity

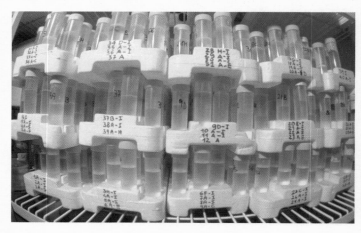

IDENTITY   All the different aspects that make a human being unique

JUDGEMENT   Decision made after weighing up the evidence. In religion, the belief in God's Judgement on human beings especially after death

JUSTICE   What is right and fair for everyone

KARMA   The law of cause and effect

KIBBUTZ   Israeli collective village based on the principles of working for the common good and shared ownership

MESSIAH   In Judaism, the one to be sent by God to bring in God's Kingdom on earth; in Christianity, Jesus Christ was the Messiah

MOKSHA   Liberation from the continuous cycle of birth, life and death

MYTH   Traditional story that contains ideas or beliefs about ancient times and events

NATURAL DISASTERS   Incidents in the natural world, such as earthquakes and floods, which often lead to large-scale death and destruction

NEVE SHALOM   Means 'oasis of peace' in Hebrew

ORTHODOX   Jews who believe God gave the complete Torah (first five books of the Bible) to Moses and who live according to its laws and traditions; in Christianity, the name given to Eastern churches, for example, Greek

PRAYER   A personal or group communication with God

PROTESTANT   Part of the Christian church which broke away from the Roman Catholic and Orthodox churches around 1500 CE

PURGATORY   A condition or state in which good souls receive spiritual cleansing after death, in preparation for heaven

REINCARNATION   Hindu belief that the soul is continually reborn in different forms – according to good or bad actions in the past (see KARMA)

RESURRECTION   In Christianity, the belief that Jesus rose from the dead. Generally, can be used to describe something brought back into activity

ROMAN CATHOLIC   Part of the Christian church which acknowledges the Pope as its head

SATAN   The Devil; the spirit of evil and enemy of God and goodness

SHARI'AH   Islamic law based on the Qur'an and the model practices, traditions and customs of the Prophet Muhammad ﷺ

SHIVA   In Judaism, a period of seven days of mourning after the burial of a close relative

SOUL   The spirit or immaterial part of human beings – the personality; often regarded as surviving physical death. In religions such as Christianity, the soul is the spiritual part of humans that is capable of being changed by responding to God

SPIRITUAL   An aspect of being human that is beyond physical description (see SOUL). In religion, spiritual relates to the sacred and the holy; the relationship with God

SYMBOL   An object, action, picture, etc. that represents an idea. It has a deeper meaning, often expressing a feeling or belief

THEIST   A person who believes in the existence of God

THEORY   Reasoning or hypothesis to explain something, for example, the theory of evolution explains the development of species

UMMAH   The worldwide community of Muslims

WAHUT AL-SALAM   Means 'oasis of peace' in Arabic

Index

Acknowledgements

Written sources

p.7 *Telling Tales* by Alan Bennett, BBC 2000; **p.9** *Harry Potter and the Chamber of Secrets* by J K Rowling, Bloomsbury 1998; **p.13** adapted from *Places and Spaces* by Wood, Logan and Rose, Nelson Thornes 1997; **p.18** 'Heroes' from *Talking Turkeys*, published by Viking © Benjamin Zephaniah; **p.21** adapted from mexconnect.com; **p.22** *both* from http://near-death.com/; **p.23** adapted from BBC News Interactive, 23 October 2000; **p.25** By kind permission of John Agard c/o Caroline Sheldon Literary Agency, 'Coffee in Heaven' from *From the Devil's Pulpit* published by Bloodaxe 1997; **p.36** A *The Times*, 23 August 2002, B *Travellers' Tales*, HarperCollins/STL 1989; **p.38** BBC Newsround, 13 February 2003; **p.46** *Letters from Mir* by Jerry M. Linenger, McGraw-Hill Education 2002; **pp.48–49** *Worlds of Difference* by Martin Palmer and Esther Bisset © WWF-UK 1992; **p.54** *Daily Telegraph*, July 1996; **p.56** *Reader's Digest*, September 2002; **pp.60–61** adapted from *Mirad, A Boy from Bosnia* by Ad de Bont © Verlag der Autoren, D-Frankfurt am Main 1994, © English translation Marian Buijs NL-Heemstede 1994; **p.69** *Six Days* by Painton Cowen, Alastair Sawday 2003; **p.83** By kind permission of John Agard c/o Caroline Sheldon Literary Agency, 'The hurt boy and the birds' from *Get Back Pimple* published by Puffin 1996; **p.90** *Taking Flight* by Anthony de Mello, Bantam Doubleday 1990; **pp.100–101** adapted from BBC News Interactive, 22 July 2000; **p.102** adapted from jabberwocky.com and shemayisrael.co.il; **p.103** *Jerusalem Post*, internet edition, July 1998; **pp.108–109** from the website of Neve Shalom – Wahat al-Salam; **pp.116–117** 'A Perfect Baby' by Tom Wilkie, *The Independent*, 17 May 1995; **p.128** *The Guardian*, 10 November 1993; **p.129** adapted from BBC News Interactive, 7 June 2001; **p.130** from globalgang.org.uk.

Photo credits

Cover *t* Index Stock/Alamy, *c* © Digital Art/Corbis, *b* © 2003 Banco de México Diego Rivera & Frida Kahlo Museums Trust. Av. Cinco de Mayo No. 2, Col. Centro, Del. Cuauhtémoc 06059, México, D.F. (photo: The Art Archive/Dolores Olmedo Mexico/Nicolas Sapieha), *background* John Townson/Creation; **p.4** *l* © 2003 Banco de México Diego Rivera & Frida Kahlo Museums Trust. Av. Cinco de Mayo No. 2, Col. Centro, Del. Cuauhtémoc 06059, México, D.F. (photo: The Art Archive/Dolores Olmedo Mexico/ Nicolas Sapieha), *r* Courtauld Institute Gallery, Somerset House, London/Bridgeman Art Library; **p.5** *l* By Courtesy of the National Portrait Gallery, London, *r* Leeds Museums and Galleries (City Art Gallery)/ Bridgeman Art Library; **p.7** By Courtesy of the National Portrait Gallery, London (photo © Derry Moore); **p.8** © Jason Hawkes/Corbis; **p.10** © Richard T. Nowitz/Corbis; **p.12** *tl* © Peter Sanders, *tr* Topham Picturepoint, *bl & br* SIPA Press/Rex Features; **p.14** Last Resort Picture Library; **p.16** National Museums of Scotland/Bridgeman Art Library; **p.19** *l* © Richard T. Nowitz/Corbis, *c* Topham Picturepoint, *r* Last Resort Picture Library; **p.20** Robert Harding Picture Library; **p.21** *tl* Index Stock/Alamy, *tr* © Lindsay Hebberd/ Corbis, *bl & br* © Danny Lehman/Corbis; **p.23** BSIP, Joubert/Science Photo Library; **p.26** Petworth House, West Sussex/Bridgeman Art Library; **p.28** *l* Circa Photo Library/© William Holtby, *r* © Joseph Khakshouri/ Corbis; **p.29** courtesy of Chandu Tailor & Son www.chandutailorandson.co.uk; **p.31** © Sonia Halliday Photographs photo by David Silverman; **p.32** *t* Circa Photo Library, *b* SIPA Press/Rex Features; **p.33** Palazzo Medici-Riccardi, Florence/Bridgeman Art Library; **p.34** *tl* Bayerische Staatsbibliothek, Munich (Cod. arab. 464, f.36r), *r* Bibliothèque Nationale, Paris/Bridgeman Art Library, *bl* The Art Archive/Turkish & Islamic Art Museum Istanbul/Dagli Orti; **p.35** © Peter Sanders/John Gullvor; **p.36** Courtesy of LifeGem UK; **p.37** *l* © Lindsay Hebberd/Corbis, *c* BSIP, Joubert/Science Photo Library, *r* Petworth House, West Sussex/ Bridgeman Art Library; **p.38** Lucasfilm/20th Century Fox/The Kobal Collection; **p.42** Will & Deni McIntyre/Science Photo Library; **p.43** *l* Penny Tweedie/Alamy, *r* Andrew Parsons/PA Photos; **p.47** NASA/ Science Photo Library; **p.56** © Peter Turnley/Corbis; **p.58** *l* Space Telescope Science Institute/NASA/ Science Photo Library, *tr* David Parker/Science Photo Library, *br* Dr Jeremy Burgess/Science Photo Library; **p.60–61** Kevin Weaver/Rex Features; **p.62** *tl* Beatrice Larco/Still Pictures, *tr* Sunset/Rex Features, *bl* © Carter Kevin/Corbis Sygma, *br* Ray Tang/Rex Features; **p.63** *tl* Olycom/Rex Features, *bl* EPA/PA Photos, *r* Rex Features; **p.68** courtesy of Rosalind Grimshaw (photo: Christopher Jones); **p.69** courtesy of Rosalind Grimshaw (photo: David Gilliland); **p.70** Circa Photo Library/© William Holtby; **p.71** photo courtesy of Joyce Miller; **p.74** *t* Olycom/Rex Features, *b* Kevin Weaver/Rex Features; **p.76–77** *all* Courtesy of Tearfund www.tearfund.org; **p.80** *l* © Bettmann/Corbis, *r* "The Lord of the Rings: The Fellowship of the Ring" © MMI, New Line Productions, Inc. ™ Tolkein Entertainment. Licensed to New Line Productions, Inc. All rights reserved. Photo appears courtesy of New Line Productions, Inc.; **p.81** *l* © HEL/Corbis Sygma, *r* 20th Century Fox Television/The Kobal Collection/Wolf, Jerry; **p.82** *l* Gil Moti/Still Pictures, *tr* *Understanding Children's Drawings* by Cathy Malchiodi, fig. 6.10 (Guilford Publications 1998) courtesy of Guilford Publications and Cathy Malchiodi, *br* Adrian Arbib/Still Pictures; **p.83** John Maier/Still Pictures; **p.84** Circa Photo Library/© William Holtby; **p.86** courtesy of Tan Books; **p.92** Ethno Images/Pierre Roussel/Alamy; **p.94** *tl & tr* © Rob Lacey/vividstock.net/Alamy, *b* Circa Photo Library; **p.95** *tl* Robert

Harding Picture Library, *bl* © Rob Lacey/vividstock.net/Alamy, *r* © Reuters/Corbis; **p.100–101** © Hanan Isachar/Corbis; **p.102** *both* © E. Simanor/Robert Harding Picture Library; **p.103** *t* © Sonia Halliday Photographs photo by Bryan Knox, *b* © Sonia Halliday Photographs photo by David Silverman; **p.104** *tl & tr* Circa Photo Library/© Barrie Searle, *bl* Sonia Halliday Photographs photo by Laura Lushington, *br* © Peter Sanders; **p.105** © Hanan Isachar/Corbis; **p.106** © Neuhaus Nadav/Corbis Sygma; **p.107** © Unger Kevin/Corbis Sygma; **p.108–109** *all* Courtesy of Neve Shalom/Wahat al-Salam www.nswas.com; **p.110** *t* Ethno Images/Pierre Roussel/Alamy, *c* © E. Simanor/Robert Harding Picture Library, *bl* Circa Photo Library/© Barrie Searle, *br* © Unger Kevin/Corbis Sygma; **p.114** *t* Courtesy of Genes for Jeans www.jeansforgenes.com, *b* Philippe Plailly/Science Photo Library; **p.115** *t* Courtesy of Genes for Jeans www.jeansforgenes.com, *bl* Mauro Fermariello/Science Photo Library, *br* Klaus Guldbrandsen/Science Photo Library; **p.118** ImageState/Alamy; **p.119** Neil Genower/Rex Features; **p.120** *tl* Patrick Barth/Rex Features, *tr* Philippe Hayes/Rex Features, *cl* Nils Jorgensen/Rex Features, *cr* John Powell/Rex Features, *bl* NASA/Science Photo Library, *br* Henryk T. Kaiser/Rex Features; **p.121** *tl* Martin Bond/Science Photo Library, *tr* © Ariel Skelley/Corbis, *bl* Garry Watson/Science Photo Library, *br* © Corbis; **p.123** *t* Topham/ ImageWork, *b* © Hulton-Deutsch Collection/Corbis; **p.124** *t* Neil Genower/Rex Features, *bl* Garry Watson/Science Photo Library, *br* © Corbis; **p.126** *t* © W. Rawlings/Robert Harding Picture Library, *b* © Howard Davies/Corbis; **p.127** *tl* Robert Harding Picture Library, *tr* © Neale Clark/Robert Harding Picture Library, *bl* Isopress Senepart/Rex Features, *br* © photo Scala, Florence; **p.128** *t* Jonathan Banks/Rex Features, *b* SIPA Press/Rex Features; **p.129** SIPA Press/Rex Features; **p.130** *all* © The Corrymeela Community – reproduced by kind permission www.corrymeela.org; **p.131** *t* © Jason Hawkes/Corbis, *c* courtesy of Rosalind Grimshaw (photo: David Gilliland), *b* Courtesy of Neve Shalom/Wahat al-Salam www.nswas.com; **p.132** *t* © Richard T. Nowitz/Corbis, *b* Klaus Guldbrandsen/Science Photo Library; **p.133** Olycom/Rex Features; **p.134** SIPA Press/Rex Features.

b = bottom, *c* = centre, *l* = left, *r* = right, *t* = top

Every effort has been made to trace all copyright holders, but if any have been inadvertently overlooked the Publishers will be pleased to make the necessary arrangements at the first opportunity.